YORKSHIRE'S FLYING PICKETS

Yorkshire's Flying Pickets

in the 1984—85 miners' strike

BASED ON THE DIARY OF SILVERWOOD MINER BRUCE WILSON

MINING HERITAGE
SERIES

Edited by
Brian Elliott

Wharncliffe Books

For the striking miners of 1984–85, their wives,
families and supporters

First Published in 2004 by
Wharncliffe Books
an imprint of
Pen and Sword Books Limited,
47 Church Street, Barnsley,
South Yorkshire. S70 2AS

Copyright © Brian Elliott and Bruce Wilson, 2004

For up-to-date information on other titles produced under the
Wharncliffe imprint, please telephone or write to:

Wharncliffe Books
FREEPOST
47 Church Street
Barnsley
South Yorkshire S70 2BR
Telephone (24 hours): 01226 - 734555

ISBN: 1-903425-51-4

A CIP catalogue record of this book is available from the
British Library

Cover design: Jon Wilkinson
Cover photographs: Brian Elliott

Printed in the United Kingdom by
CPI UK

Contents

Foreword

by Dave Hadfield ('Wingnut')
(National Union of Mineworkers)

Even though it is now twenty years since the 1984–85 miners' strike people keep asking me 'Can you remember what happened?' The answer is, quite simply 'Yes!' especially when I look back at the events noted in my own diary.

The miners' strike was a time when new friendships were formed and, sadly, when some old friendships were broken, never to be repaired. Some marriages grew stronger and some fell apart. Some mornings were cold and some were hot. But we did find out who our real friends were.

The majority of people who were not directly involved in the dispute always ask about Orgreave or wherever a mass picket had taken place. Such events, and many others, will stick in my mind forever.

At the start of November 1984 the Silverwood NUM branch decided that the committee should think about organising Christmas parties for the children. These took place on 15 December for kids up to the age of nine and on 22nd for those children from the age of ten to sixteen. The women's section organised all the food and arranged the catering. What they did was to ask local butchers and bakers for donations of meat, pies, bread and cakes. Myself, Keith Lockley ('Corgi') and Brian Ripley, all branch committee men, were asked to see about getting donations of toys and finance from local businesses, and this was achieved. I contacted twenty-two local CIU clubs and received a financial donation from each one. I even sent a letter, with a stamped addressed envelope, to the Rotherham Conservative Club but never received a reply. At least that was ten out of ten for trying!

The two parties were a great success and the tradition continued until 1994 when Silverwood closed. It was the last pit to finish under nationalisation (NCB) prior to what was left being sold back into privatisation.

The Silverwood Branch of the National Union of Mineworkers can be proud of sticking to the policy of the Union; and we must always remember the 3,000 Nottinghamshire NUM members who did not cross picket lines.

Finally, I would like to say that without sticking to your principles you have got nothing.

I am proud to have been associated with the striking miners of Silverwood, their wives, families and communities during the great strike of 1984–85 and I am delighted to write this Foreword in support of the book.

Dave Hadfield ('Wingnut')
South Yorkshire NUM Branch Secretary (Silverwood NUM committee, from 1983 & Delegate,1990–1995/branch closure; NUM member 1970–present).

Introduction

Brian Elliott

The diary of former Yorkshire miner Bruce Wilson of Rawmarsh, near Rotherham, offers a remarkable insight into the daily life of a flying picket (and his crew) during the 1984–85 miners' strike. Here, and perhaps for the first time, we have a day to day and totally honest account of what it was like for a group of active young miners supporting their union and fighting for jobs and communities during the longest and most bitter industrial dispute of modern times.

Bruce and his Silverwood pit mates, Shaun Bisby, Darren Goulty and younger brother Bob Wilson were joined by Cortonwood miner Bob Taylor. From the outset it is clear that they got on very well together, enjoying each other's company and quickly establishing roles, even mock 'titles'. Bruce's elderly Triumph 2.5 was the trusty 'battlebus' that conveyed them on so

Police with shields at Orgreave on 'Bloody Monday', 18 June 1984. Arthur Wakefield

Mounted police ride through the streets of Orgreave, 18 June 1984. Arthur Wakefield

many journeys into the coalfields of Nottinghamshire, Derbyshire and Yorkshire. How they and so many other pickets managed to evade so many roadblocks and barriers was a remarkable example of both ingenuity and determination, often against overwhelming odds. Quoted in the *Financial Times* of 4 March 1985, the Chief Constable of Nottinghamshire stated that 164,508 pickets were 'turned away' during the first twenty-seven weeks of the strike. No doubt our five pickets formed part of this official statistic but – like many others – minor roads, tracks, even open countryside provided alternative routes of 'getting through'. Police manning during the strike was unprecedented. There were 1.5 million deployments of police from 43 forces, according to figures published in the *Financial Times* at the end of the strike. The peak occurred during clashes at the Orgreave coking plant near Sheffield when 8,100 officers were used in one week's orchestrated policing.

The NUM officials at the strike centres did what they could to co-ordinate and organise teams of pickets, issuing instructions, providing petrol money, support and advice. But, in many instances, the police via surveillance, information and other means were in a position to deploy men and set up roadblocks, particularly into Nottinghamshire where many miners

Veteran miner Arthur Clayton at the abandoned Cortonwood colliery, autumn 1985. Soon all the buildings would 'disappear' from view. Brian Elliott

continued to work. Writing about the miners' strike in her recent autobiography, Stella Rimington, the former Director-General of MI5, tells us that the 'picket lines and miners' support groups were not our concern', denying any deployment of 'agents' or of 'telephone interceptions'. However, in the next sentence she says that 'investigations' did take place 'of those who were using the strike for subversive purposes'. Was this a mischievous reference to the NUM leadership or particular area officials? Maybe one day the full and definitive story will come out.

In normal circumstances some of the actions of Bruce and his mates were offences that really did deserve arrest and punishment. But throwing missiles, setting traps, ignoring police instructions and the like should be seen within the context of an exceptionally bitter dispute. The first-hand accounts of clashes with the police and a variety of eyewitness accounts of brutality, at the very least, helps us to appreciate situations that really were battlegrounds, situations in villages such as Brampton functioning under siege conditions.

Former Cortonwood miner Bob Taylor takes a look at the remains of the old pit site, now occupied by MacDonald's restaurant, B & Q and Morrison's supermarket, October 2003.
Brian Elliott

In January 1985 I swopped a classroom in a Barnsley area comprehensive for a small adult education office at Wickersley Comprehensive School. My new job was to organise and promote adult and community education, a remit that soon extended to Maltby, and also to Ravenfield and Thrybergh (towards Dalton), so in a real sense Silverwood Colliery was on my doorstep. It was a very challenging task and would be increasingly so in the aftermath of the strike. Individuals and groups, especially women, did take up new learning opportunities in a variety of settings and locations. Later that autumn I had an unofficial tour of Cortonwood Colliery in the company of an eighty-four-year-old former miner. The site had just been abandoned. We felt as though we had boarded the *Mary Celeste*. Tools and papers were strewn in workshops and offices and graffiti was testimony to mining humour: *Come on Down … the Price is Right* written in chalk on an old workshop door. It was a sad and eerie feeling. Morrison's supermarket and other modern commercial buildings now occupy most of the site.

Queen Mary takes an unusual ride on a railway trolly at Silverwood as part of the royal visit to industrial Yorkshire, 8 July 1912. Rotherham Archives & Local Studies Library

This advertising card printed by the NCB in the early 1970s, refers to Silverwood Colliery as one of Yorkshire's 'million-tonners', producing over a million tons of coal a year, one of the region's most modern pits. Bruce Wilson Collection

A contingent of Silverwood miners celebrate the extraction of one million metric tons of coal (from the Swallow Wood seam) when the pit had a workforce of 1,342. South Yorkshire Coal. Annual Report 1985–86. Jeff Poar/NCB

Many collieries closed and were quickly obliterated from their local landscapes in the years following the end of the great strike. This pattern continued with further haste after the shock Heseltine announcement of 1992. My work was then in the old mining village of Dinnington, near Rotherham, in a building that originated as a mining and technical college. Not long afterwards I was involved in some of the partnership work in providing opportunities and training for young people and adults at the former Kiveton Park Colliery offices, a wonderful building full of character. English Heritage became so concerned about our vanishing mining heritage in 1994 that it commissioned an aerial survey of the deep-mined coal industry. In Yorkshire, the Prince of Wales Colliery at Pontefract closed in 2002 and the end of UK Coal's Selby Complex this year will leave just five deep mines in Yorkshire: Kellingley, Maltby, Rossington, Harworth and Hatfield Main; with only a handful of others elsewhere. Concerns, warnings and predictions made by the NUM in the early eighties can not be argued with given the present state of our privatised coal industry. The present Labour government has come to the rescue of British Energy, responsible for nuclear powered electricity. According to figures

Silverwood achieved record-breaking tonnages, duly celebrated and promoted by British Coal in the aftermath of the strike. Jeff Poar/Bruce Wilson Collection

from the Department of Trade and Industry, the domestic production of coal was exceeded by imported coal for the first time in 2001. Coal is now imported into Britain from Poland, South Africa, Columbia, USA and Australia. In the not so near future we may even have to rely mostly on imported gas for electricity generation. Who would have thought this would happen twenty years ago?

Silverwood Colliery was sunk to exploit the famous Barnsley Seam by the Dalton Main Collieries Ltd between 1900 and 1905; and also linked to the nearby Roundwood Colliery which operated until 1931. Silverwood quickly became one of the largest mining concerns in the Yorkshire area. In 1909 it was already employing 2,593 men underground and 635 on the surface where there were extensive workshops, a wagon repair shop and a sawmill. The installation coking ovens, part of a considerable array of by-product facilities, along with a

HEADING INTO THE FUTURE: Silverwood miners celebrate new developments at one of the most successful collieries in Yorkshire. Jeff Poar/Bruce Wilson Collection

brickworks, made the Silverwood site, located between the villages of Ravenfield and Thrybergh, an impressive industrial complex, so important that King George V and Queen Mary included it on their itinerary to Yorkshire in 1912. For many years annual output from the 'Barnsley' exceeded one million tons and, after nationalisation, the poorer quality Meltonfield Seam was also developed. From the 1950s until the early 60s the NCB instigated a major reconstruction programme at Silverwood. Soon afterwards, the Swallow Wood Seam was successfully developed. When the NCB chairman Lord Robens paid a visit to the colliery in 1967 it was regarded as one of Yorkshire's ten 'long-life' pits and coal from another

Celebrations at Silverwood, 20 January 1990, when almost £2,500 was raised towards the BBC Children in Need appeal. Bruce Wilson collection

traditional Yorkshire seam – the Haigh Moor – would soon be added to the colliery's production potential. By the 1970s production was concentrated on Swallow Wood, particularly from development in the Braithwell district workings. The quality coal was in demand for coking purposes by British Steel and the the power stations (CEGB). Despite the strike, Silverwood miners went on to achieve remarkable production records, including the fastest 1 million metric tons in the area. In the spring 1992 a £10 million investment was planned in order to develop the Parkgate Seam in the wake of Silverwood achieving a record annual output of 1.4 million metric tons. The Parkgate scheme never started, the pit closing, on 23 December 1994.

Two years ago I was fortunate in working with veteran Yorkshire miner Arthur Wakefield in order to publish his much acclaimed 1984–85 strike diary. I never thought that within such a short period another 'forgotten' Yorkshire pitman's journal would appear. Working with Bruce Wilson and meeting his friends over the last twelve months has been a marvellous experience. Hopefully, the book will add to our knowledge and understanding of one of the most eventful periods in modern British social and industrial history.

Setting the Scene
by Bruce Wilson

At the beginning of the strike it was like a long holiday 'free from the pit'. But when the summer came, all those pasty-faces disappeared! replaced by fit and sun-tanned men. Although it was a lovely summer, we did not lose sight of the purpose of it all. The sense of humour, the comradeship was always there – we were all mates – we were all miners, striking miners, fighting for our jobs and our communities. Today, in job requirements, there is great emphasis on 'team-work' but back in 1984 we had it all.

As the dispute wore on and we were still picketing and flying all over the country we began to get 'battle fatigue', going to Silverwood Miners' Welfare in the evenings for our 'orders', hoping things would be OK, and that we would get home safely following our picket duty. After several months of activity I was beginning to want a rest. I was glad when Christmas came but soon developed itchy feet again, missing the excitement of it all – of trying to beat

Pickets walking back from duty at Harworth. Darren Goulty salutes the cameraman (Bruce Wilson). On Darren's right is Mick Bush and (just out of shot). Bob Taylor

the roadblocks into Nottinghamshire and trying to get to Clipstone Colliery, the 'Fort Knox' of the Notts coalfield: to dodge and duck and dive, to weave in and out of the Nottinghamshire countryside, and to see the faces of the police when arriving at Clipstone – it was dedication to duty if you got there. The look of bewilderment on the picket police faces when you arrived and stood across from the pit gates was something I will never forget. It was all well worth it. My forefathers had fought and died in two world wars so that I could live in a democratic society so nobody was going to pen us in Yorkshire. The police could take our names and turn us back but we were not put off by such undemocratic tactics.

Although we were, for a variety of reasons, unable to become flying pickets straight away, when we did get our team together we soon made up for it. I was the driver, my brother Bob the co-pilot and there was Bob Taylor, Daz Goulty and Shaun Bisby in the back, all Silverwood men except 'Captain' Bob who was from Cortonwood colliery. Our NUM Secretary, Granville Richardson, put us on to him as he lived near us, in Rawmarsh, but couldn't get to his own pit as he had no transport.

The lads decided that my nickname should be 'Commander Bond'. I had the strategic job of planning routes the night before picketing, looking for country lanes, farm and old railway tracks and so on. Bob Taylor soon became our 'Captain'. Our sense of humour, determination and comradeship rolled all adversity and hardship out of the way. I feel that we did not lose the strike, we did not lose our pride – just out livelihoods. Miners are hardworking, adaptable people. Just look at the lads' faces, pictured walking back from picket duty at Harworth colliery, the smiling faces and friendship and the unity. Maybe it was naive innocence but whatever it was, it was not manufactured or bought, something that many of the politicians of the time did not appreciate. We were born into mining, moulded by our environment and working conditions; and so were our communities. We were like a big family: all miners. My old car became the 'battlebus' and other pickets got to know us and would hoot their horn and wave as we went down the motorway. We would even get comments about bats flying and circling around the ancient roof.

We were a small team of self-styled commandos: 'Yorkshire Flying Pickets', consisting of:

'Commander Bond': Bruce Wilson (driver)
Captain: Bob Taylor
Co-pilot/navigator: Bob Wilson
Back seat pickets: Shaun Bisby & Darren 'Daz' Goulty

My strike diary
My diary entries were honestly written, a few dates may be slightly out but the accounts were written immediately after each day's events or a day later at the most. Events described are as they happened, as they were seen by me and my 'crew'. I don't want to say what is right or what is wrong, as readers can make their own judgement about the strike. My diary, photographs, press cuttings and souvenirs of the strike were kept in a cupboard for almost twenty years.

Getting it published
In the summer of 2001 I took my daughter, Suzanne, to a mining exhibition at Clifton Park Museum in Rotherham. To my amazement, there was a vast array of memorabilia from my old

pit, Silverwood Colliery, even including a 'COLLIERY VACANCIES' sign which used to stand outside Deployment office. Faintly etched on the sign was the name of the first scab to go back to work during the strike. I don't think that the museum staff had noticed this 'historical bit of graffiti', but I was able to point it out to them. I also asked if the museum might be interested in some of the Silverwood and strike items that I had saved. Judy Ely was pleased to accept donations from me of several brass plates of manufacturing details etc, salvaged from the underground locomotives that I used to drive. I also gave the museum a variety of 1984/85 newspaper cuttings and a full set of the 'strike issues' of the *Yorkshire Miner* newspaper. Judy

Bruce and his 'crew' back at Orgreave after almost twenty years: (left to right) Bruce Wilson, Bob Taylor, Darren Goulty, Shaun Bisby and Bob Wilson. Brian Elliott

The flying pickets assemble again at the old Orgreave railway bridge: (left to right) Darren Goulty, Bruce Wilson, Bob Taylor, Shaun Bisby and Bob Wilson. Brian Elliott

told me that they had little information about the miners' strike, so I mentioned the diary that I had kept, a more or less day by day account of picketing. She wondered if I had thought about having the diary published. Well, I smiled, and thought who would ever want to know about the strike, almost twenty years ago; but she assured me that there would still be a lot of interest.

My conversation with Judy Ely set me thinking so I went to see Tim Brannen at Rotherham Library. He told me that there was nothing much local on the shelves concerning the miners' strike.

Somewhere down the line I got talking to Philip Caplan of Philip Howard Books, Rotherham. Phil was kind enough to read through my notes and then recommended that I contact Wharncliffe Books of Barnsley as they were well-known publishers of local books. It was Wharncliffe who then put me in touch with their commissioning editor, Brian Elliott who arranged to meet me. After looking through all the material, including photographs that I had taken and ephemera that I had collected, Brian recommended to Wharncliffe that the book should be published, hopefully in time to commemorate the twentieth anniversary of the 1984–85 strike.

I had also let Ann Thompson and Ann Whitehouse of Rawmarsh & Parkgate History Group have a look at some sample pages of the diary. After reading it they exclaimed, 'It's true!' meaning that all that they had heard about the strike was correct. That set me thinking as well. It did look as though, despite the passage of time, people would be interested in what I and my mates had to endure over a twelve month period; and what it all meant to families and mining communities.

My wife, Gay, fully supported me and looked after our young kids during the strike, and never moaned once. Heartfelt thanks are also due to 'my crew': Bob Taylor, Bob Wilson (my brother), Darren Goulty and Shaun Bisby. It was a pleasure to serve alongside them in my car and on the picket lines. It was great when we got together, with Brian Elliott, for a memorable reunion, in June 2003 – for the lads, my lifelong friends, it was our first group meeting in nineteen years. Brian was able to interview each crew member so as to obtain their individual and independent views about the strike. He also took us back to Orgreave and Harworth so that present-day photographs could be taken. I am also very grateful to the written contributions, memories and support of Bob Taylor and NUM official Dave Hadfield ('Wingnut'); and also not forgetting our local union officials including Granville Richardson, Stuart Tennant and Eric Cassidy – and all the Silverwood lads. Additional photographs and memorabilia were also kindly loaned to myself and Brian by my crew members.

In my dedication to the book I refer to all striking miners but I also feel that special tribute should be made to the striking miners of Nottinghamshire and Leicestershire who were in the minority during the long struggle.

Thanks are also due to our supporters who gave so generously during the strike: for example, the teacher who gave us a bag of apples when we were on picket duty and the hard-up housewife who put a few coppers in our collection tin. There were many, many more kind people who supported us from all walks of life.

I would like to say a special thanks to Brian Elliott, for his editorial skills and hardwork; and for his unwavering intention to see my diary published. Without his help and interest, a lot of our social history would be lost. Now, future generations will have the opportunity to appreciate what life was like as a flying picket during the 1984–85 miners' strike.

There were very many other Yorkshire pickets who were as active or even more active than myself, in fact several lost their lives, many more suffered injuries and illnesses, had marital problems, were imprisoned and lost their jobs. Hopefully, my diary and comments will show what a good number of us experienced twenty years ago. It seems like yesterday.

A full list of acknowledgements is listed towards the end of the book, in Appendix 4, but both Brian and myself extend our sincere apologies if we have missed anyone

Brian Elliott (editor left) with Bruce Wilson (diarist) and 'Ben' the dog, Rawmarsh, Chirstmas 2003.

out. Picture credits/acknowledgements (where known) are also shown after each caption.

One day our grandchildren may ask 'What were coal miners?' and 'What happened to them?' Maybe they will even dig deeper and pose the question, 'What did my grandad do in the miners' strike?

I hope the final answer will be: 'He was a striking miner.'

Bruce Wilson, February 2004

Picket Profiles

by Brian Elliott

Based on a series of independent interviews,
November 2003

Shaun Wayne Brian Bisby

> *It may have been a defeat for the miners but it was not a defeat of our principles.*
> *I am proud of what we stood up for – and just look what the NCB and*
> *Government did to our pits afterwards. We were right all along.*

Shaun was born at Canklow on 12 September 1960, one of three children from the marriage of Albert and Irene Bisby. He attended Rotherham's South Grove Comprehensive School, leaving at the age of almost seventeen to find employment at the Non-Ferrous Melting Company. However, by the time he was eighteen, in 1978, Shaun had started work at Silverwood Colliery. He recalled that the wages were better there and that it was a lot easier to get a job at the pit in those days. Following training at Manvers, Shaun worked underground, looking after the conveyors and on supplies. It was while assisting with the underground locomotives that Shaun came into contact with regular driver Bruce Wilson, six years his senior. The two miners soon became good friends.

When the strike started Shaun lived at East Herringthorpe with his first wife and five-year-old daughter, Maria. He agreed fully with going on strike and it seemed a natural process for him to join ' my mate Bruce' and go picketing, something which, despite some of the scrapes and dangers, he thoroughly enjoyed doing – well most of the time! He was always supportive of Bruce's antics, especially in always trying to get into Nottinghamshire. There were numerous occasions when his sense of fun and good humour was replaced by understandable self-preservation when escaping from charging police at Orgreave and elsewhere; but it was important, Shaun told me, 'not to get detached from your mates as the snatch-squad might catch you'.

When I asked Shaun about the low point of the strike year he had no doubts: it was when more and more miners started drifting back to work, even one or two at his own pit. Despite his own financial hardship, with little more than £9 a week for his young family to live on, he would have stayed out even longer.

Like his picketing friends, Shaun did not find the atmosphere when returning to work after the dispute to be a very happy one, leaving Silverwood for good in 1987. A training course for bricklaying followed, and then a two-year stint working away from home, on the Channel Tunnel project. Since then, Shaun has worked as a warehouseman for Exel Logistics and lives at Catcliffe. His front room contains a good selection of family photographs, including a large framed image of eleven-year-old son, Ryan, who, judging by the medals also on display, is a successful young footballer. Shaun will never be ashamed of his achievements during the 1984/85 miners' strike because he, like his picketing colleagues, fought for what he believed was right.

Shaun Bisby in his Catcliffe home, 2003. Brian Elliott

Darren 'Daz' Goulty

Victory or defeat ? We'll it was mixed. It was a victory that
we stayed out so long but I would have stayed out even longer
given the chance.

At just eighteen-years-old at the start of the strike, Darren Goulty was the baby of Bruce's 'commandos', born in Hollybush Street, Parkgate on 29 May 1965. Darren's father, Brian, was also a striking miner, a face-worker originally from nearby Stubbin Colliery, and later Silverwood, so the Goulty family were very hard hit during the twelve month strike. After leaving Rawmarsh Comprehensive School, aged sixteen, Darren spent a few months working at Texas Home Care, prior to starting his mining education and training at Manvers. As a young lad at Silverwood, he worked underground, as a conveyor attendant, track-layer,

Darren Goulty displays a framed collection of miners' checks, 2003. Brian Elliott

Darren Goulty watches four policemen walk down the road at Newstead Colliery, Nottinghamshire.

haulage hand, pump packer and also assisted the dinters levelling the roadways. The strike was a few weeks old before Darren decided to go picketing, jolted into action after watching miners being treated badly on television news programmes. He went picketing with 'some other lads' from the pit but stayed with Bruce as he found the experiences 'more exciting'; and because 'the commander' always tried to get through, despite the blockades.

Darren's most worrying moment took place near Thrybergh when he was walking down the hill, away from Silverwood Colliery, when, with his friend Craig Dimbleby, was forced to walk on the pavement between parallel lines of police who belted both of them with truncheons and shields – just because they were striking miners.

Bob Taylor at the Cortonwood Colliery memorial pulley wheel, Brampton, October 2003.
Brian Elliott

When Darren went back to work he found that the friendliness had gone and that it was a difficult situation, having to work near some men who were strike breakers. On one occasion he was almost dismissed, accused of intimidating a scab. He carried on, working at Silverwood until 1993, not long before the pit closed, but he was pleased to finish.

Darren has no regrets regarding his role as a flying picket and is the proud owner of a good collection of strike badges, framed by his father, kept alongside an array of checks from local pits.

Robert 'Bob' Taylor

*You know, Brian, I am not normally 'a hooligan' but we all had
to do what we could to fight for our jobs, and some of the
events, and some of the the ways we were treated just made my
blood boil.*

Bob lived in the Blyth Road area of Rawmarsh during the strike but his family came from Parkgate, his father, Ken, finding employment at the local steelworks. Coal mining, however, was also in his family. Albert, his paternal grandfather, worked at Aldwarke Main Colliery and his other grandad was a boy miner at Warren House, subsequently awarded the BEM for first aid work in the steel industry. After leaving Haugh Road Secondary School, Bob worked for a short time as a trainee joiner but decided to apply for a job at his local pit – New Stubbin – since his mates were earning better money there. His first job was on the pit top, loading tubs with wooden props and supplies. Following training at Manvers, he was employed underground on haulage work, tramming material to the districts and the coal faces. In 1971 he married and tried his hand working in the steel industry, at the River Don works, but moved back to mining, starting at Cortonwood Colliery in January 1979, one of the pits that sparked off the 1984 strike. Divorced, living with his parents in Blyth Road, and feeling betrayed by the Coal Board and Thatcher's Conservative government, Bob was determined to support his union one hundred per cent, joining Bruce Wilson's emerging small team of flying pickets. At thirty-two he was the oldest of the self-styled 'commandos' and a very distinctive figure, due to his ever-present flat cap and then ample build; and the only non-Silverwood man.

For Bob, the most frightening moments during the strike include being dragged by a sympathetic Treeton resident into his home so that he could hide behind a wardrobe – along with fifteen other pickets! pursued by an angry police riot squad; chased by the cavalry at Orgreave; and chased by a 'blood-thirsty' group of Nottinghamshire scabs who had disembarked from their bus near Pye Hill, the last incident still resulting in battle-like flashbacks. Perhaps Bob's funniest moment was the expression on the face of the curious policeman who looked in the back of Bruce's 'battlebus' and saw Bob wearing nothing but wet underpants, following a picketing mishap, when a stream had not been quite successfully negotiated.

Like the other pickets, Bob did not find the atmosphere too good when he returned to work at Cortonwood. When the pit finally shut, in 1985, he was transferred to Silverwood Colliery which he felt was 'like coming home'. He remained there until taking redundancy in September 1993, not long before the pit closed. Bob remarried after the strike and now works part-time, for First Line, the Rotherham bus company.

Bob Taylor was a participant in the remarkable (2001) re-enactment of the *Battle of Orgreave*, staged by Jeremy Deller for Artangel and filmed for Channel 4 television. He maintains a strong interest in local coal mining history. Given the choice, Bob would still like to be a coal miner.

Norman Bruce Wilson

*I did not see the miners' strike as a defeat
because we stood up for what was right and we fought
for our right to work in support of our Union, our families
and our communities.*

Bruce Wilson, by coal tubs at the National Mining Museum for the North of England (former Caphouse Colliery), Wakefield, November 2003. Brian Elliott

Bruce Wilson at the Humber Bridge, following picket duty at Gunness Wharf, Scunthorpe, July 1984.

Norman Bruce Wilson was born in the Parkgate area of Rotherham on 3 September 1954. His father, also named Norman Bruce, worked in the hot and dusty environment of the Templeborough Melting Shop, dying of respiratory problems at the age of sixty-two. The Wilsons were a family of five boys and two girls. Bruce junior left Haugh Road Secondary School at the age of seventeen, in 1971, and started a British Steel apprenticeship at his father's place of work. He left the industry towards the end of 1977, working for a few months in holiday camps in Torquay where he met his future wife, Gay, a north London girl. They married in 1979 by which time Bruce had already had a spell of training and underground work at Silverwood Colliery, a situation which became more permanent from the autumn of

1978. Underground work, typically included a variety of jobs, from supplies, development work and 'dinting' to a regular role as a locomotive driver. During the strike, when Bruce turned thirty, he lived with his wife and two young children, in a former pit house at 3 Coronation Road, Rawmarsh. Gay and Bruce had just taken a mortgage for their property when the strike began.

Bruce told me that the best moments during the strike were when 'his team' were 'all together in the car and on the picket line', and when supporting their union, the National Union of Mineworkers. There were some occasions, Bruce recalled, such as going to Doncaster in the autumn of 1984 when he wondered if he and his friends would get back home without injury. A similar frightening situation was when police charged through the streets of Orgreave and Brampton (Cortonwood). Our civil liberties, said Bruce, '…went to the wall – you had to be continually alert and also have your wits about you or you could be cut off from your mates and snatched.' Lighter moments were many and various, most notably when he steered through, around or bypassed those 'impossible' roadblocks – much to the consternation of the police. Steve McQueen would have been proud of him. One of the low points for Bruce was when picketing his own pit, often 'getting hammered' in sight of a few men who had returned to work, men who he believed would have been supported by their union if they had asked for help; but it was also a time when the support from local people – schoolteachers, nurses and members of the public who would arrive with complimentary bags of food, fruit, even portions of chips – was so meaningful to him and his mates.

Returning to work after the strike, Bruce felt strange, and at times intimidated. He believed that some men had 'blanked everything off as though we had only been away a weekend.' It was not long before things 'got back to normal', though the atmosphere was just not the same. Losing interest, his mates leaving, and following a period of sick leave, redundancy was accepted in February 1988, from 'a pit that had lost its identity'. A variety of jobs followed, including a period of self employment and qualification as a Class 1 HGV driver. In recent years Bruce has worked as an agency driver of articulated lorries, for a variety of companies, delivering to depots nationwide.

Bruce has developed an interest in coal mining history, especially in relation to his old colliery and the 1984/85 strike.

Robert 'Bob' Wilson

> *To me, the strike was a great achievement because of the length of time*
> *we stuck it out, having to live on the limited resources, and surviving*
> *against adversity.*

Born on 26 November 1957, Bob is one of Bruce's younger brothers. Leaving school at the age of sixteen, he worked for two years in farming, on the Wentworth estate. This was followed with a similar period of employment for Rotherham MBC, tractor driving and working on building sites. The prospect of better wages at Silverwood Colliery resulted in work there from the age of twenty, following the usual training at Manvers. Bob's underground mining experience, like brother Bruce's, was eclectic, 'doing a bit of everything, laying roadways, dinting, working on supplies and eventually driving diesels.'

Bob shares a joke with a policeman at Cresswell, July 2003.

During the strike Bob was single, living at 12 Green Peace Cottages, Upper Haugh. His girlfriend and future wife, Debbie, worked in the local strike centre. Bob, with his infectious sense of humour, was the biggest joker of the group. And that says a lot! He immediately responded to Bruce's invitation to go picketing, looking forward to 'having something to do', and 'getting out and about' – as well as getting the £1 picket money. Even his new dog, a Lakeland/Jack Russell terrier, was named 'Striker'. Bob felt that the best moment of the strike was in June, at Orgreave, when deploying 'home-made smoke bombs' against a convoy of lorries getting into the steel works, amid a huge police presence. In contrast, during a 'push' at Pleasley, he feared for his life, squashed against a line of policemen and almost suffocated. His funniest recollections included the incident where Bob Taylor lost his ever-present cap and got soaked in a stream; and when brother Bruce drove into a farmer's gate post, a 'hello

Bob Wilson in 2003, Brian Elliott

hello' police officer almost immediately banging on their car window. A low point was when his cottage was burgled, when he was out picketing.

When asked his opinion of his older brother, Bob had no doubts, paying tribute to Bruce's determination and positive attitude – and driving skills – during the strike, saying, 'He was a guy who never gave up, despite all the odds. We were a good team, Brian.'

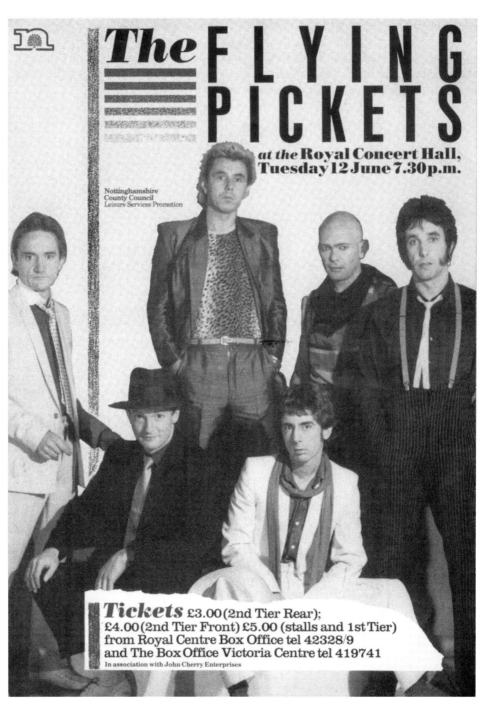

The 'Flying Pickets' pop group were very supportive to the miners during the 1984–85 miners' strike.

I
Forming my Crew and Mobilising the Battlebus
March–April 1984

'… we were not allowed to go about our business in a so-called free country.'

Darren Goulty displays a victory signal from the back of the 'battlebus', somewhere in Nottinghamshire.

EDITOR'S SUMMARY

The shock announcement, on 1 March 1984, of the NCB South Yorkshire Area Director Geoffrey Hayes' decision to close Cortonwood Colliery is generally regarded as the spark that ignited the great coal strike of 1984–85. However, matters were more deep-rooted. Miners at nearby Manvers were already on strike and a national overtime ban had been in operation for five months. The NUM Yorkshire Area ballot in 1981, which resulted in an 86% majority in not accepting the closure of any pit unless on grounds of exhaustion, was to become a key platform for the justification of subsequent action. The appointment of Ian MacGregor, the former trouble-shooter at British Leyland and British Steel, as chairman of the National Coal Board, on 1 September 1983, was a political decision seen by many as a Tory strategy to reduce the power of the miners following the successful strikes of the 1970s and the fall of the Heath government. Hayes' 'perfect solution' to reduce capacity (via redundancy and transfer) was understandably outrageous to a colliery workforce who had been recently assured of a good five years employment and who had faithfully implemented a millions pounds worth of development work. It was a particularly devastating 'welcome' to the miners transferred to Cortonwood following the closure of Elsecar Colliery only three weeks earlier.

By 15 March only 21 of 174 British pits were 'working normally' and the first tragedy occurred when a young Yorkshire picket, David Gareth Jones, was killed outside Ollerton Colliery in Nottinghamshire. A massive police operation, involving the deployment of thousands of officers, and strategically-placed roadblocks, took place in Nottinghamshire where the majority of miners continued to defy the NUM recommendation not to cross picket lines.

This was the context in which Bruce Wilson begins his strike diary.

Bruce describes the meeting held at Silverwood Miners' Welfare, known locally as 'The Baggin', with an apt contribution from Cortonwood miner Bob Taylor who was soon to join Bruce's crew of young flying pickets. The diarist describes what was to become a familiar pattern for thousands of pickets over the coming weeks and months: obtaining secret instructions from the strike centre followed by journeys into Nottinghamshire and North Derbyshire, avoiding if at all possible, the police roadblocks.

On 9 April 100 miners were arrested in Nottinghamshire and Derbyshire in some of the worst disturbances of the strike todate. Two days later, a NACODs' (National Union of Deputies, Overmen and Shotfirers) vote in favour of strike action did not achieve the required two-thirds majority and on the 19th an NUM delegate conference in Sheffield voted against a national ballot.

Returning to Bruce's diary, his final entries for the month of April relate to a mass picket at Cresswell and the use of Merseyside as well as South Yorkshire police at Bevercotes. We also have more than a glimpse of the humour and antics of five young men on a mission in a 'battlebus'.

THE DIARY

Saturday, 2 March

Have been on nights, working down the Braithwell district, probably my last shift before the strike starts. I had started at six on Friday evening. I am a loco driver. I was working with Shaun Bisby, who was a loco guard. Fetched the men out, took the loco to the pit bottom garage. We talked about tomorrow's meeting and the possibility of a long strike, then made our way out, finishing work at about 2 am.

Sunday, 3 March

Meeting at the Baggin (Silverwood Miners' Welfare). It definitely looks like a strike, an indefinite strike. It's a shame, we have only about a week's coal left at home and my delivery

Bob Taylor (wearing cap) walking back from picketing at Harworth, 23 April 1984. On Bob's right is Lol Scales and behind (left to right) are Shaun Bisby and Mick Bush.

Miners assemble outside Sheffield City Hall at a special NUM delegate conference, 19 April 1984. Several Silverwood men are pictured in the lower right corner of the photograph. NUM

SILVERWOOD COLLIERY,
NATIONAL COAL BOARD,
SOUTH YORKSHIRE AREA
Produced by NCB Public Relations (Yorkshire)

Layout of the underground workings at Silverwood Colliery, showing the Braithwell area. NCB

is due on 4 March. The feeling of some of the men that I have spoken to is to work but the Union recommends industrial action. Always back your Union. Without them you are lost. I will back the Union. At the meeting it was packed out. A very good case was put forward in favour of the Union recommendation. A couple of miners put their hands up and argued for continuing to work and everyone listened to the views expressed. When it came to the vote my hand went up in favour of action, probably the second to do so, then many other hands went up. The recommendation was in favour of industrial action. I heard that one Silverwood man had tried to commit suicide due to the overtime ban. He was up to his neck in debt with a new house and may do it proper now.

Gay, my wife, is poorly in bed and remained so during the first week of the strike. I helped to look after our two children, my baby daughter, Suzanne, who is six months old and my son, Ricky, aged three years. I was suffering from an infection on my left knee, a massive boil and couldn't walk for a fortnight. Dr Venkit, from Parkgate came to see me and gave me a prescription for antibiotics which cost our lass £3 in cash. Never normally see a doctor unless it's serious.

'Captain' Bob Taylor describes his early experiences and feelings at the start of the strike.

The news came through that my pit, Cortonwood, was to close. When I arrived at work I was gobsmacked, really angry. So were the rest of the work force. Men from Elsecar colliery had been transferred just six months earlier, mainly the older lads who had five years left to do. Elsecar colliery at Hoyland had closed due to its working life ending. The NCB had told the Elsecar men that Cortonwood had five years life left. So what went wrong?

The union meeting, Sunday morning, 3 March

Everyone who worked at Cortonwood was in attendance. I remember Mick Carter (NUM official) putting the case for industrial action and I listened to his every word very carefully. One hundred per cent of us voted to fight the pit closure, and I was determined to do what it takes even if it meant stopping out indefinitely. We all knew the media and the world would be watching us. When the meeting was over and we came out the cameras were there. I was on the national news for three seconds!

The official picket at 'The Alamo', Cortonwood Colliery, in January 1985. Brian Elliott collection

At the end of the pit lane we built a big cabin and inside it we placed old busted settees, springs sticking out all over. That was our comfort for the coming months. We all knew that if the pit shut it would be the end of the community. This was to become known as the 'Alamo'.

Thinking about it, I knew I was on strike but I was one of the lucky ones. By that I mean I was fortunate living with my parents, with a roof over my head, no rent to pay and no food problems. If I had been living on my own I might have finished up sleeping on a park bench. The only income I received when on strike was £1 a day picket money, nothing else, other than an occasional food parcel. *But no matter how hard things got I would not cross that picket line.*

I live on the outskirts of Cortonwood, at Rawmarsh, which is about three and a half miles from the pit. At the start of the strike I used to walk to the Alamo picket everyday and stand with my mates. I didn't get a chance to be a flying picket at my own pit but some of the lads I know who worked at Silverwood Colliery told me to go to the Baggin (Miners' Welfare) in Dalton on the Sunday and have a chat with Granville Richardson, the Union man. It was Granville who fixed me up with Bruce, a lad from Rawmarsh who had a car and who I was to go flying picketing with for twelve months.

I remember the first morning with Bruce when he picked me up about five. I was tense, not knowing what I was in for. I'd heard rumours of what can happen on picket lines, between the flying pickets and the police. We picked up two more lads, Bob, who was Bruce's brother, and Shaun Bisby from East Herringthorpe, Bruce's mate. We went to the Baggin first to meet the rest of the flying pickets and got our orders for the day, and our destination, in Nottinghamshire. Leaving the strike headquarters, we noticed a police patrol car watching how many cars were leaving. I suppose they would radio and warn other police to watch out for us. We didn't get far down the motorway before we were stopped by the police and turned round, telling us to go back. And they say this isn't a police state.

Anyway, Bruce asked us if we wanted to go home or try and get through another way. We agreed to go ahead. Sod 'em. We finished up driving down a country lane, trying to beat the roadblocks. We tried to make it to Pleasley, border country, but there were police everywhere. We gave up that morning and came home but never mind, tomorrow's another day. My first day with Bruce'e team was over.

Every time we got to Pleasley there was a roadblock on the corner, so on this occasion Bruce had a bright idea. He suggested we got out of the car and walk over a field and then he would meet us further down the road as he thought he might stand a better chance of bluffing his way through on his own. Four of us made our way through the field, climbed over a barbed wire fence and tried jumping over a stream. I was a bit heavier than the rest of the lads so when I jumped I landed in the water, about two foot from the edge. Bruce was in hysterics, he just couldn't stop laughing. Can you imagine the verbal I gave him?

Sometimes, when we arrived in Nottinghamshire, and after doing our picket, we would go somewhere else and make a day of it.

I remember on one occasion, at Ollerton crossroads, Bruce would say to us 'Get down! Police and roadblocks are in front'; but he left us crouching down the bottom of the car for a good ten minutes, saying 'Stay down', even when it was all clear. He thought it was very funny, but we all had to laugh as well.

I think it was about the sixth time that I went on the road with Bruce when the Yorkshire area had made arrangements to meet somewhere near Pleasley on the South Yorkshire/Derbyshire

Police blocking the road at Cresswell. Arthur Wakefield

border. If we got through Pleasley there was a good chance of getting into Nottinghamshire; and if not, falling back to Cresswell or somewhere else. We reached our destination OK though. The Union men were talking to us down the road where we were to start our march from when, suddenly, we came to a stop. In front of us were police, loads of them. Some were in riot gear, forming a blue wall. Anyway, we carried on, getting closer to the blue wall, chanting as we walked, **'UNITED! UNITED! THE MINERS WILL NOT BE DEFEATED'**. It was a great sound and sent a shiver down my spine and the hairs at the back of my back stood on end; but it was also very frightening, not knowing what was going to happen. In fact it came to blows, every man for himself. Batons (truncheons) and fists flying all over the place. The men in blue were after blood. It opened my eyes, as I was brought up to respect the police, but did not do so anymore. That day I came home unscathed, and lucky, unlike some of my battered mates.

THE DIARY (continued)
Sunday, 15 April
A few days earlier, while working on my car, Mick Tracy or 'Red Mick' as he was also known, asked me why I was not out picketing. I explained to him about my bad knee and that each Sunday I went to the Baggin to see what was going off. I decided to put my name down to go picketing. So me, Bob Wilson, 'Daz' Goulty and Shaun Bisby got our first flying picket duty, destination Bolsover, Derbyshire the next morning. The pit had 900 men and 400 of them were on strike.

Monday, 16 April
Got up very early and went round knocking my mates up till I had a full team. Set off to Bolsover. At first I could not believe what was happening. Roadblocks all over. Went by Roche

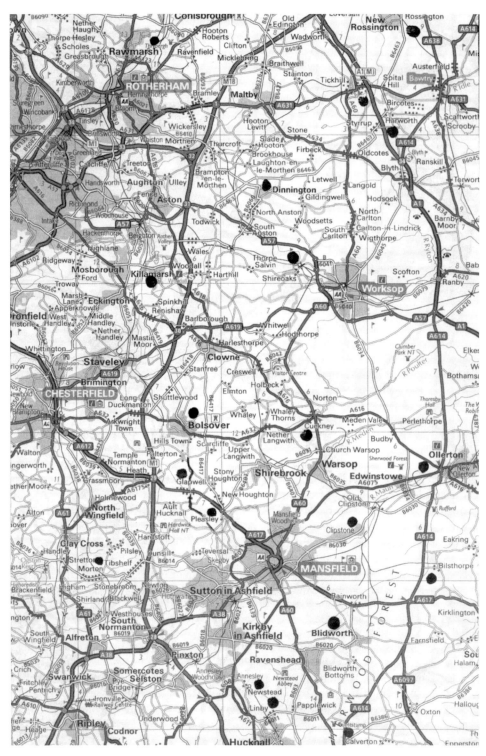

This map, marked with sites of Notts/Derbys collieries, was used by Bruce and his team of pickets when planning routes.

44

Abbey, but we were stopped by a policeman in a Jaguar car and made to turn back. He followed us from Oldcotes crossroads until we reached the South Yorkshire sign and then left us alone. We did not give up. Still managed to get to Bolsover, via Dinnington, arriving about 5.15 am. It was cold and raining, pretty grim, barbed wire everywhere, not just to keep sheep in, and there was a massive police presence. Hung around for a bit and noticed something strange – miners shouting at the scabs, then moving to the rear of the pickets. They were smartly dressed, very clean cut, wearing new donkey jackets, looking just like they had just walked out of Foster's menswear shop. Found out later that they were *agent provocateurs*!

It was a fairly quiet morning there so we decided to move on to Welbeck and got through OK; but the police wouldn't let us anywhere near the pit gates. A copper told us that anyone shouting the word 'scab' would be arrested. It was Surrey police this morning. They tried penning us in. Bob Wilson came close to being nicked as he gave it some 'Baaa! Baaaa!' despite the warnings. Walking back to the car, our names and addresses were taken down by the police. The police seem to think that us drivers are fair game, just nick the driver and the rest of the lads will have to go home. Bastards.

Tuesday, 17 April

Orders for today – Ollerton, Notts. Picked team up and set off through Maltby towards Oldcotes crossroads where we were stopped by the police and – here we go again – our names and addresses taken. Gave them some verbal since we were not allowed to go about our business in a so-called free country. The police just smirked at us and told us that we were not going anywhere fast. Started to drive back 'helped' by a police escort which accompanied us to the South Yorkshire boundary sign again. Felt like royalty for a while, like a motorway jam sandwich, due to the police escorting us. Didn't give up. Found another way into Worksop but we came to a standstill, loads of cars being turned back, so had to call it a day. Returned to Silverwood Miners' Welfare, had a cup of tea and read a few newspapers, then dropped off the lads. Felt a bit guilty as the NUM were giving me petrol money and I only put half in the tank as we were struggling to get through the roadblocks.

Wednesday, 18 April

Orders for the day – Nottinghamshire again. Set off in the morning. I got a tenner, £9 for petrol and £1 for picket money. Tried all ways to get there but only got as far as Worksop because of the heavy police presence. There were hundreds of pickets' cars turned back. So far the police appear to have Notts well and truly sewn up.

Tonight, as a joke, I found an old bronze swimming medal, complete with its ribbon. I put some **Coal Not Dole** stickers on it (they are yellow with black print) and this was to be our Deed of the Day award, always to be kept on the car dashboard. Bob Taylor won it the most, awarded for 'conspicuous bravery' for a day or up to a week. We had some laughs over the medal.

Thursday, 19 April

Got our orders from the Baggin as usual, the previous evening. Always called there about 6 pm, to find out the next day's destination and collect petrol and picket money. Linby pit in Nottinghamshire was the target. Me and Shaun set off down

An original Coal Not Dole *sticker.*

45

The 'Police State' poster, published by SOGAT (printers' union) on behalf of the NUM.

the M1 but at every junction after leaving South Yorkshire there were police blockades. We got off at Junction 25 and were turned back as expected and a police Jag followed us back up the motorway, but they must have seen our 'Police State' poster in our back window. We had picked up a hitch-hiker, a lad from Middlesbrough. He didn't believe what was happening but has seen it for himself now. The police in the Jag looked a bit upset and they zoomed away as soon as we reached South Yorkshire. Went back to the club for a cup of tea, then dropped Shaun off and made my way home. Did not need all my £9 petrol money again but it will save for later. Reported to the Baggin at teatime. It's Linby again tomorrow.

Friday, 20 April

Set off for Linby colliery. Still novices, we went down the M1 again, didn't know any better. Pulled off at every junction down to 25. On each occasion the police stopped us and searched our car boot. At the last junction we went up the slip road and we were stopped and asked to get out of the car and asked our names and addresses. One bobby opened the car boot and when he closed it left his black leather gloves on the boot lid. He asked me if I'd forgot my gloves, the one's on the boot. I said they were mine and, quick as a flash, got back into the car – with a new pair of black leather gloves to my name. Don't wear them but they served as a trophy – and there will be a bobby somewhere with cold hands.

Monday, 23 April

Got orders from the Baggin, destination Harworth colliery, near Maltby. When we arrived, it was a mass picket, there must have been 10 -15,000 pickets and thousands of police. There were a few arrests.

Tuesday, 24 April

Same again, Harworth, getting there at 4.30 am. There were Bob Wilson, Bob Taylor, Shaun Bisby and myself. It turned out that we were the decoy, only thirty pickets got through, including us. The police were Eastenders, from London (Thames Valley) and right bastards.

Wednesday, 25 April

Today's orders – Cresswell, North Derbyshire. A mass picket. There must have been 10,000 pickets there and 2,000 police. Loads of trouble, all hell let loose at times. The police would only let so many pickets' cars through, so as to find out where we were going, then they sealed the roads, concentrating their resources where needed.

Thursday, 26 April

Bevercotes colliery, Notts. Managed to get through. There were 2,000 pickets and Merseyside police and South Yorkshire police with horses. A scab had his windscreen put through. An old man, near us, wanted to go to the toilet but the police told him to do it where he was standing. We were surrounded by the police. The elderly miner made his way to some bushes and two coppers followed him. One of them smacked him, the other dragged him off and he was arrested.

II
Nottinghamshire and Orgreave
May 1984

'Bloody hell, the noise was deafening.'

A quiet day at the British Steel coking plant at Orgreave. Catcliffe and Rotherham can be seen in the distance. Bob Taylor

EDITOR'S SUMMARY

By early May 1,479 striking miners had been arrested and a mass picket involving several thousand miners had taken place at Harworth. Bruce and his crew spent the first two-weeks of the month dodging the blockades and getting through to picket in Nottinghamshire, at Pye Hill (where they encountered police from South Wales), Welbeck, Ollerton, Pleasley and Bevercotes. On 10 May they were able to visit Berry Hill, the Nottinghamshire Area NUM headquarters where they met the local leader, Henry Richardson. For a fleeting moment or two the crew were 'caught on camera', shown on television news footage, holding up 'Police State' posters. The third week of May was spent away from home, 'billeted' in Nottingham where they were able to vent some of their feelings to a secretive Ian MacGregor and pickets at Babbington Colliery, including a mass turn-out when Merseyside police were encountered once again. On 14 May a mass rally had taken place in Mansfield involving an estimated 40,000 marching and demonstrating miners. Two days earlier, a Women Against Pit Closures demonstration had taken place in Barnsley, about 10,000 in attendance. Bruce and his crew continued their picketing journeys into Nottinghamshire, but from their home base, but the emphasis switched to Orgreave towards the end of the month. NUM leaders met Ian MacGregor for talks on 23 May but the discussions ended on the same day.

Meanwhile, coke convoys had started to leave the Orgreave depot, near Sheffield, bound for Scunthorpe. Consequently, a gradual build-up of pickets took place, NUM President Arthur Scargill making a rallying speech to his troops at Orgreave on Bank Holiday Monday, 28 May, a quiet day, when no lorries appeared. The next day was not so quiet. Bruce describes some of the incidents and pitched battles that took place in the vicinity of the coke depot, some of the worst since the outbreak of the twelve-week strike, with police wearing full riot gear. There were 82 arrests and 69 reported injuries and estimated 7,000 pickets. The crew returned to Orgreave the next day, 30 May, which, with a mounted police charge, was almost as eventful, the young pickets even witnessing a 'copper' disguised as a picket. Much to the delight of the media, it was also the day when Arthur Scargill was arrested and charged with obstruction.

THE DIARY
Thursday, 3 May

Orders for today – Pye Hill pit. I've heard it has only 14 months to go, almost exhausted. Set off in the morning and got through OK. Turns out to be a mass picket. South Wales bobbies. OK! We got there first but the police put us all in a field and surrounded us. Went for a game of cards in the village pub, a nice little country pub, near the pit entrance. Later, there was loads of trouble and some arrests. The locals seem to be 50/50 for and against the strike. When we first arrived a local lady almost jumped into the car to pat us on the back when she realised we were pickets.

Friday, 4 May

Pye Hill again. Got there without any trouble. I think they were only letting us through as we were quiet, probably keeps us busy, leaving other Notts pits alone. We keeping walking around the village, looking to see where the scabs come from etc and get to know the area. We have got friendly with a commanding police officer with pips. He shouldn't underestimate us. Everyday he says good morning to us. He likes the situation, quiet and no trouble. But we are getting bored and may have to do something about it.

Monday, 7 May

Welbeck Colliery. Got through OK, and so did a few hundred other pickets. The police must have overlaid. About thirty of us walked towards the pit but the coppers arrested the first four pickets that they laid their hands on. One of the arrested lads had already been turned back in his in car but had stopped further up the road and walked it to the pit. We surrounded the police and gave them a lot of hassle and the arrested lad got away. The coppers saw him again and arrested him for a second time! Police blocked the road further up and forced us back. Had enough, so we decided to go to Cresswell but there was no chance today – and the same for Harworth. The police had got the roads and area well and truly sealed.

Tuesday, 8 May

Orders for today – Ollerton, Notts. Don't know how we managed to get there but we did even though the police would not let us out of the car, though Ollerton's a no-go area for flying pickets. We decided to make our way back to Cresswell, North Derbyshire. Only a few hundred pickets and a small police presence. A few miners walked in to work and we gave them some scab. One of them started to walk in and then threw his snap into the pickets, turned around and went back home! Bloody hell, the noise was deafening. The next one walked in and it all went quiet. I shouted loudly and slowly, 'You scabbing bastard!' but the man looked unnerved, and glanced sheepishly over his shoulder. He did not know what was gong to happen, it was still deathly quiet. He turned round and went back. I heard him say 'Fuck that!' I then drifted into the middle of the pickets, a wise move. I could see the police edging their way to where I had been standing. If I had stayed put they would have got me.

Police turning back pickets on the A614 near Ollerton. News Line

They would not dare go into the middle of us. Afterwards I made my way back to the car, watching my back all the way. Back to the Baggin for some dinner, beans and egg.

Wednesday, 9 May

Met at Baggin this morning, 8.30 am. Every car was full. Left for the leisure centre at Killamarsh. Got there early and had a game of football, then a meeting at the WMC, just up the road. We left for Hucknall in a massive convoy. Got to Pleasley but it was full of coppers. Some local lads guided us through country lanes. About thirty to forty cars got there and there was a big picket on. The pit was in the town centre! One clever copper, about seven foot tall, got a young lad and pinned him against a garage door and threatened him. I've seen that bobby around once or twice since.

Thursday, 10 May

Destination today Bevercotes pit but made our way to Mansfield where there was an anti-strike demonstration by Nottinghamshire miners. When we were given our orders it was stressed that we should picket peacefully. Couldn't get through to Bevercotes as there were police road blocks all over. We were sealed off. Made our way to Pleasley Miners' Welfare Centre, situated on a slight hill, high off the road. All the lads went inside. Had a cup of tea and some sandwiches and waited until about 7.30 am until the rest of the pickets arrived. When we moved out there were, bloody hell, hundreds of coppers who had come from nowhere. They had the bottom end of the road blocked off, hundreds of them. Set off marching down the road but they would not let us through. We tried charging but they got their truncheons out and started to charge us. We split into two groups and tried to get round them but no chance. We had no leadership. Our group was forced back up a narrow dirt track, back towards the Welfare. The police were striking anyone who did not get out of the way long enough. We got some right hammer. They wanted us to run back towards the welfare but, even though we got some truncheon, we did not run. The film crews were told to switch their cameras off at the sights going on. Got back to the welfare and had to stand on the grass, off the road, before we were totally surrounded. We decided to get on a bus but the police got on and threw us off. Stood back on the grass again, surrounded by police. Another bus pulled up in front of us and again the police got on board and turfed any pickets off. We were held at the welfare for ages, before eventually being allowed to make our way home.

We decided to still try and make it to the Mansfield demo. A local lad told us how to get there by avoiding roadblocks. Made our way to the M1, towards Junction 29 but at Glapwell turned off at the Clay Cross signpost, then sharp left down a country lane, passing Silverhill Colliery and Sutton pit. Finally got to Berry Hill, Mansfield, the Notts NUM headquarters. The staff there gave us a cup of tea and we met their President, Henry Richardson. He was wet through with sweat and gave us another cup of tea and some Notts NUM badges. He has a very difficult job in the circumstances. It was a real eye-opener, visiting Berry Hill, situated in a pleasant area with landscaped gardens. It's another world down here.

PS. Some Silverwood lads were on film – Me, Shaun, Albert Parker, Gary and the rest. I was seen holding a 'Police State' poster and so is Shaun but his poster was upside down!

Friday, 11 May

Early start today, to Bentinck, Notts and got through OK. Had to walk half a mile to the pit though. While making our way a lad passed us, swinging his snap bag. As he got near us some pickets asked him if he was going to work but before he could answer he received a smack

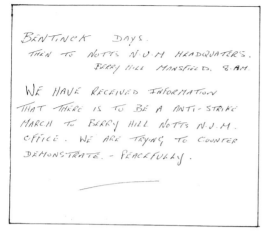

BENTINCK DAYS.
THEN TO NOTTS N.U.M HEADQUATER'S.
BERRY HILL MANSFIELD. 8.A.M.

WE HAVE RECEIVED INFORMATION
THAT THERE IS TO BE A ANTI-STRIKE
MARCH TO BERRY HILL NOTTS N.U.M.
OFFICE. WE ARE TRYING TO COUNTER
DEMONSTRATE. - PEACEFULLY.

Original 'Orders for the Day', given to miners at the Silverwood Miners' Welfare ('The Baggin') prior to flying picket duty.

and he set off running towards the pit, crying. The lad that assaulted him, and his mates, dispersed quickly. The pit entrance was on a slight hill to the left of us. There must have been a couple of hundred of us that got through. Those scabs that got in were mostly young – the selfish little bastards – they go in, confident and smile when they pass the pit gates, sheltered by all the police. I was stood at the front of the pickets, on 'the front line' when suddenly somebody shouted 'ZULU!' and everybody pushed and shoved from behind. I remember having my face pressed against a policeman's cheek. I couldn't breath and thought that I was going to die. I only weigh ten stone. Good job they stopped pushing as I thought I would be a gonner. Everybody eased off and thinned out but it took me several minutes to come round, walking about as though I had been on the beer. Had an unsteady walk back to the car and returned to the Baggin where I had something to eat and drink.

A 'scab', protected by the police, going in to work at Bentinck Colliery, Nottinghamshire.

The great march and rally through Mansfield on 14 April 1984. NUM

Banners held high and all vantage points taken at the Mansfield rally and demonstration, 14 April 1984. Arthur Wakefield

Bob Taylor recalls the demonstration at Mansfield and a week 'billeted' in Nottingham, 14–18 May

It was a fantastic feeling at the Mansfield demo. There were thousands of miners, their wives and children there, all marching with banners and there was not much trouble. I will always remember one of the Union men asking us if we wanted to go and stay in Nottingham for five days. We agreed straight away. I had mixed feelings about it, excited but also apprehensive, knowing that we were going to stop in the middle of enemy territory. We drove to Nottingham after the demonstration.

Four of us were sat around this table in a pub. Some of the locals overheard us talking and realised we were striking miners from Yorkshire. One lass started making her mouth, saying that *The Sun* says this about the miners, *The Sun* says that, getting my blood to boil, knowing as I did that this newspaper thought we were the scum of the earth. Felt a bit better, though, after a couple of pints. Wasn't used to a drink, being on strike with no money for beer. On the first night we were in sleeping bags on the floor. Next morning I was aching all over, my stomach, back and legs feeling very painful. I was just coming round when 'Big Alan' (Alan Wilson) came over and apologised for kicking me during the night, as he thought that I was *his* sleeping bag, as he got back late, and the lights were off.

Off to Babbington Colliery on the Tuesday, arriving with plenty of time to spare. When they arrived for the day shift we shouted 'SCABS!', 'SCABS!'. Nothing doing then until the afternoon shift when it was the same treatment again. We returned to our digs and had a short sleep.

It was a rather quiet week, unofficially collecting on behalf of the NUM at dinner times.

Friday came and some students informed us that Ian MacGregor, the Coal Board boss, was due in the town centre, so all five of us went there and waited for him. We didn't have long to wait. He got out of his car, and glanced over towards us and gave us a look of dismay but one of the lads jumped into the middle of the road, shouting 'WE WILL NEVER SURRENDER, YOU BASTARD!' whereupon three men in blue started walking towards us. As they got closer I could not believe how tall they were, I've never seen police so big. We didn't stay long. We heard about MacGregor's visit on the radio later, edited of course.

THE DIARY (continued)
Monday, 14 May
Thirteen of us stayed with students in Nottingham. The Silverwood men were:

> Bruce Wilson
> Bob Wilson
> Bob Taylor
> Shaun Bisby
> Mick Bush
> Alan Wilson
> Stuart Tennant
> Jeff Hammill
> Steve Hammill

After the demo, I asked Mick Tracy to inform our loved ones that we were stopping in Nottingham for a week. The first night we stayed at a house in Sneinton, thanks to young lass who had been on the demonstration. She was a supporter of the Socialist Workers' Party but her house was like a tip. Boxes and piles of newspapers filled the rooms. During the day, when we weren't picketing, we stopped at the Polytechnic and the pop group Prefab Sprout were performing there; but at night we stayed at a local unemployment centre which opened specially, at 10 pm for us.

The first day there I treated the lads to a meal at the Poly (using spare petrol money that I had saved from my picket allowance) but we felt rich men as the NUM officials now gave us £5 per day picket money, with drivers' getting an extra £5 for petrol, so I received £10 a day.

Tuesday, 15 May
Myself, Mick 'Bushy' and Shaun went to the Victoria Centre in Nottingham. Mick had a bright idea. We bought a cheap plastic bucket, covered it in *Coal Not Dole* stickers, and went collecting for the NUM strike fund. We'd only been at it for ten minutes when we bumped into Steve Hammill, an NUM official who wasn't very pleased, telling us that what we were doing was illegal, but we managed to get a few more stickers from him. It wasn't long before we had collected £8. Later, you should have seen us, sat in a pub, eight pound's worth of shrapnel on a table, with our plastic bucket hidden in an M&S bag underneath the table (though you could still see the stickers through the plastic). I had a guilty conscience but it was just what we needed as we had no money – the troops had to be fed; and we even managed to put Queen

on the juke box as well. During the collecting we got a lot of hassle from the locals – we were cheeky bastards, collecting in Nottingham town centre – but we also got some well wishers. One lady put 50p in the bucket, after, that morning, she had seen police treating women on the picket lines badly. One woman, whose husband was a scab, gave us 50p! An old man called me 'a dirty Yorkshire sod' and I was told to 'piss off back to Yorkshire'. A policeman came up close and watched but he did not hear me mutter 'You bastard'.

Wednesday, 16 May
Still picketing, Babbington, a mass picket this morning. Some Silverwood lads got chased. The coppers would probably have arrested them for going through gardens but the rest of the picket shouted ' leave them alone' and they did. The police were 'scousers', from Merseyside and had been OK up to now.

Thursday, 17 May
Frank came round to see us. He's been a striking Notts miner from Cotgrave Colliery and has been showing us around the area. 5 am – picket duty at Babbington, all sodding day. Did the early shift and went for breakfast, but couldn't really afford it. Back at 11 am for the afternoon shift. Very boring. Just stood there, shouting 'Scab' but the police like it when it's fairly quiet, it's easier for them. Back to the Polytechnic for dinner. Sat across from five or six young lasses and got talking. One of their fathers is a scab! We explained to them as polite as we could that none's job is safe. Her's was, though. She worked in a factory making knickers for Marks & Spencer. We told her that if the NCB gets its way then all the Yorkshire women won't be able to afford to buy knickers, so she could be made redundant. You can't really talk to someone who just won't listen.

Friday, 18 May
Babbington again. Found out that MacGregor was at a meeting in Nottingham town centre. The *Royal Hotel*? Set off walking there and met some other lads walking back from the centre who told us he'd gone. Went back to the Poly but someone told the NUM Secretary that MacGregor was not supposed to be leaving until 11 am, so we ran back. He was still in a meeting, so we couldn't have timed it better. Got him coming out. If we had arrived earlier we would have been moved. He got out of his car, glanced towards us and gave a look of dismay. Next minute one of the lads jumped into the middle of the road and shouted 'WE WILL NEVER SURRENDER, YOU BASTARD MacGREGOR!' We all joined in then, shouting 'MacGREGOR! 'OUT! OUT! OUT!' from our position round the corner, out of sight. There must have been a thousand bobbies there. Three of them started walking towards us and as they got closer they got bigger. Big bastards they were. We scarpered fast, in fact I have never seen Alan Wilson run so quickly. We were on telly that night,

Ian MacGregor, chairman of the National Coal Board.

on ITN, BBC and *Calendar*, as 'famous' as MacGregor. Made our way back to our digs – the unemployment centre. Thought we should have a clean up, wash and shower etc, all thirteen of us. One problem – we only had one towel! Everyone had a shower, myself, Bob Taylor and Shaun were last in. Someone threw Captain Bob the towel. What did he do with it? Well, he put one hand in front of him and the other behind and did a forward and backward movement with the towel, drying his naughty bits. Me and Shaun dried ourselves with our vests. Bob threw the towel at us but we were too quick for him.

After an eventful afternoon we made our way back home to Yorkshire, good old Yorkshire. There was nobody to stop us leaving Notts but they didn't like us getting across their boundary. When I sometimes see the Woodall Services sign on the M1 after picketing I know it is 'Welcome to South Yorkshire', or 'The Socialist Republic of South Yorkshire' as Margaret Thatcher might call it – and it's nice to be on our way home. Dropped Bob Taylor off at Rawmarsh Baths and opened the car boot to let him get his clothes out but when he picked up his purple nylon underpants up someone's toothbrush was sticking to the crutch area. No one would claim ownership.

Monday, 21 May

Thoresby Colliery, fall back to Cresswell. Managed to get through. We are getting better. When we get to a road block the lads duck down and keep quiet. I just look forward, drive, and try to look indifferent, hoping they will take me for a local. Drove past Ollerton pit gates! Tried to get through to Thoresby. Saw a roadblock, so turned round but it did not work this time – coppers chased us and stopped us, taking all our names and addresses. Told us that the next time we are seen in Nottingham we would be arrested, clever bastard. We were told to piss off back to Yorkshire. I drove on. We should not have been spoken to like that by the police. We went up and down country lanes, and then reached another bleeding road block, bobbies stopping all cars. I turned round again and they chased us again! When they caught up with us, got a police escort to the Derbyshire border by a police car and a motorbike bobby. We felt like royalty! Managed to fall back to Cresswell where there were a few hundred pickets and a small police presence. Gave it some scab when the workers arrived and then made our way back to the Baggin and had some egg and beans. It's about time they changed the menu! One Yorkshire picket told me a lad had a hole in his petrol tank and had a note placed on his windscreen saying ' Hole in your petrol tank', from a sympathetic scouse bobby. Ah well.

Tuesday, 22 May

Meeting at Silverwood Miners' Welfare at 9.30 am. Our destination: Silverhill Colliery, Notts. Set off and ought to have known better as we were turned back at Pleasley but persevered and finished up going down a back alley – local residents must have thought we were gangsters. There was only just enough room for the car to get through the alleyway. After this we came to yet another road block but got through, the lads getting down in the bottom of the car; then we saw another road block! Lucky it was a dry day as we came to an old favourite of ours – a disused railway track and embankment so drove along it for several hundred yards not knowing where it would lead but the gamble paid off, the road blocks were beat. Managed to get within a mile of the pit gates but the road was blocked yet again by the police. We stayed for about an hour but no luck, the police did not ease off. Didn't fancy walking a mile and leaving my car at their mercy. Went back to Cresswell instead. There were a few pickets present so we stayed there and gave the scabs some abuse. On the way back at the sight of every policeman or roadblock that we came across I sounded my horn to attract their attention and we shouted abuse at them with a few rude hand signals, 'wanker' being the favourite, just to make sure they got the message from a car full of pickets. Came to one road block and the lads were supposed to be hiding in the bottom of the car but as I glanced around I could see a lone hand stuck up, visible to the police, with two fingers displayed. The police were not very pleased.

Wednesday, 23 May
Today's target, Sherwood, near Mansfield. Got £5 petrol money. Left Baggin at 9.30 am. Couldn't get through but managed as far as Shireoaks. We had heard that Shireoaks was being picketed by women and children. Went down country lanes towards Shireoaks but no chance at getting close to the pit, all the access roads well and truly sealed. The police wouldn't even let us walk as we were regarded as illegal secondary picketers and were supposed to only picket our own place of work. Made our way back to Cresswell, arrived about 11.55am but too late for the afternoon shift going in, so made our way back home.

Thursday, 24 May
Busy day today. Met at Baggin, 9.30 am, destination Bevercotes. Managed to get through and within a mile of the pit. Went through Harworth, Serlby Hall, Retford, then A1. Police refused to let us through again. As there was a lot of us we gave them some 'flying wedge' and they responded by trying to push us up the road. A senior police officer pulled out a cosh and hit a picket on the head. The poor lad, from Cortonwood pit, fell like a stone. Coppers then stuck the boot in. He finished up with a massive gash to his head. He held on to Pete Bailey, from Silverwood, with both hands. Suffering from shock, an ambulance came to collect him about half an hour later. Pickets wouldn't let the police look after him as they would also arrest them as well. Paul Burke (a Silverwood miner) was like a dog sniffing for a bone, looking for a brick. Afterwards, we doubled back to Harworth, parked in a pub car park and walked in two's: me and brother Bob, Shaun and Captain Bob. Two coppers let Bob Taylor and Shaun through. Me and our kid told them that we were going to the pub up the road and the police warned us that if we were seen picketing it would be an instant arrest. We walked into the pit entrance but missed all the action again. Walking, I made our way back to the car and the others followed. Saw Bob 'W' and Shaun give a police van some 'zeig heil', accompanied by a Nazi salute. They turned round and threatened us with arrest, taking all our names and addresses. Clever Scottish copper; he looked at my car and threatened me. His gaffer told us that if we were seen at the pit tomorrow it would be an instant arrest. We told him 'all right, but we will be coming back anyway.' Went back to Baggin for some snap.

Men are going to Orgreave from the Baggin this afternoon. Another £1 petrol money plus £1 picket money. Conveys of lorries taking coke to Scunthorpe. When we got to Orgreave there were too many police. When the convoy arrived some pickets broke away and bricks were rained on the lorries, about 4–6 having their windows put through. When they came out again, about 24 lorries this time, me and Bob, with Shaun, ran to a wall near the road when one lad jumped over the wall on to the causeway but all the coppers caught him and knocked him about a bit. All he was doing was shouting. Some of the police jumped over the wall and chased all three of us, usual routine : bobbies helmets off, place them on the floor, and set off charging after us. They had no chance with full uniforms on. It was a hot day. Only chased us for about two hundred yards, then they gave up; but then another 20 of them attempted another chase. One bobby shouted, 'GET THAT BASTARD IN THE BLACK LEATHER JACKET' (Shaun Bisby). We came to a factory at the bottom of a banking, next to the Parkway. Some lads at the top (who worked there), overlooking us, shouted encouragement to us, saying 'DON'T LET THEM GET YOU.' The police shouted to us 'COME ON DOWN LADS, WE'RE ONLY GOING TO ARREST YOU.' We replied 'FUCK OFF!' There was a hole in a fence that we came to so we scrambled through and were safe. There must have been a couple of thousand bobbies at Orgreave today. I took my jumper off and walked back to the car, didn't want to be recognised, and then picked the lads up. Lucky today!

PICKET LINE SCUFFLES. 13 ARRESTED FOLLOWING FIGHTING AT BEVERCOTES PIT WHERE 3,000 PICKETS GATHERED. SEVERAL POLICE OFFICERS INJURED AND TAKEN TO HOSPITAL. POLICE SAY 100 PICKETS AT WELBECK AND SIMILAR NUMBER AT OLLERTON BUT NO ARRESTS REPORTED.

Stop Press information provided the latest news about 'picket line scuffles'.

The police on duty today: at Bevercotes – Notts police
at Harworth – West Midlands police
at Orgreave – South & West Yorkshire; & Hampshire

Later on, at Bevercotes, I heard that Paul Burke, the Silverwood lad, got arrested again. Shaun never wore his black leather jacket again after today.

Friday, 25 May
Orgreave today. Getting into a routine now. Shift times for pickets at Orgreave: 7am to 12. 30 pm (starting days) and 4pm to 5pm (starting afters). Cold this morning. Pickets split into two groups, 50–100 men in each. The first run came early, at 12.00. Went back at 4pm but did not see anything. Throwing it down with rain and got soaked so went home after a long day. On the slip road onto the Sheffield Parkway four windscreens were put in, which made our day. The drivers are scabs. Lorries mostly covered in, some signs say 'BSC' but several named 'Holme on Spalding Moor'.

ON THE MOVE: Lorries at Orgreave.

ON THE MOVE.. WITH CONVICTION

● A LOT of the trucks which are carrying coke through miners' pickets at Orgreave to the British Steel works at Scunthorpe are owned by a company which has been convicted of corrupting British Steel officials at Scunthorpe.

A British Steel spokesman at Scunthorpe told me that "about a third" of the lorries moving coke from Orgreave belong to Consolidated Land Services.

He said that the firm did a lot of other work for BSC as well.

Saturday, 26 May
Working Saturday, a bit different, 12 am to 6 am. The scouting shift. Got to Scunthorpe, with Bob Taylor, about 10.40 pm. Saw this large pub at a roundabout so we called in for one. It was about 2–3 miles from the steelworks. When we walked in the room was huge, you couldn't see the end of the bar! It

Consolidated Land Services (CLS), according to this news report, were responsible for transporting a good deal of Orgreave coke to Scunthorpe, despite a recent conviction.
The Sheffield Star

was also packed, everyone sitting down. Some locals came up to us – they knew we were striking miners – and bought us a drink and 20 fags. It still felt very intimidating as there must have been hundreds of people and it was fairly quiet. The locals were friendly but we were glad to leave. Got to Appleby Frodingham about 11.30pm and just missed the evening shift. I didn't have a clue as to what we were looking for. I think it was the movement of lorries but it was a rare night out for me and Bob. It was cold and wet at the steelworks entrance. Someone had left a fishing umbrella so put it in the car boot and moved to the next entrance but was moved on by the police. They were from Humberside. Had a look around but nothing doing, so set off home at 5.30 am.

Monday, 28 May

Bank holiday today. Reported for duty at Orgreave, 8 am. There were about 2,000 pickets there. Arthur Scargill was there too and he gave a speech. Came home about 9.30 am as there were no lorries because of the bank holiday. Will be back tomorrow. To Silverwood Welfare tonight, 7 pm. Reputedly 50,000 tons of coke at Orgreave. Weather today cold and drizzling. Lads at Scunthorpe reckon it's a firm called ELS doing the coke runs.

This newspaper report illustrates some of the scenes that Bruce and many other pickets witnessed at Orgreave on 29 May 1984.

The NUM President Arthur Scargill being arrested at Orgreave on 30 May 1984. The senior officer is Superintendent Nesbit. Phil Spencer/News Line

Tuesday, 29 May
Battle for Orgreave
Before going to Orgreave this morning we went to Bentinck Colliery, Notts. Pickets outnumbered the police (from Hampshire) but we couldn't wait to get to Orgreave. Got there later this morning and it wasn't long before heavy fighting broke out. We laid in wait to ambush the convoy of lorries, same place, a slip road off the Sheffield Parkway – in the wood at the top of the embankment. When the lorries arrived, the scene could have been taken from the film *Sparticus*: all hell let loose. It rained bricks and stones. Windscreens were smashed again. Made our way back to the rest of the pickets on the lane and there was a line of police in front of us and plenty of 'Here we go, here we go'. Then it was 'Zulu'. In the crush I went down on the ground. Shouts of 'ARE YOU TAKING ANY PRISONERS, Mr SIMPSON?' (number 1 bobby at Orgreave) were heard.

Wednesday, 30 May
Battle for Orgreave: Day 2
In the morning we set off for Annesley, Notts but the police wouldn't let us through, so fell back to Bentinck where there were only a handful of pickets. Set off for Orgreave and there

was heavy fighting again when we arrived. Same as yesterday. There was a strange sight this morning – several policemen chased a copper disguised as a picket, caught him in a field, kicked the shit out of him and didn't believe him when he told them he was a policeman – until he got to hospital.

Thursday, 31 May
Set off into Nottinghamshire this morning, forgot where exactly we were heading but stopped by police near Hardwick Hall, not far from Silverhill Colliery. Advised to turn around and go back. We did – but back to Orgreave. Gave it some 'Zulu' on the front line. Lovely day, warm weather so just had my vest on. After a while I just sat down and watched, enjoying the scene. Police sent the cavalry forward, again and again. I saw myself on telly later, now wearing a blue jumper and a blue and white striped shirt. It was quiet in the afternoon.

III
𝓑𝓵𝓸𝓸𝓭𝔂 𝓞𝓻𝓰𝓻𝓮𝓪𝓿𝓮
JUNE 1984

'Shortly after the first push the long shields parted and out rode 14 mounted police straight into the pickets. As they did so police beat on their shields with truncheons creating a wall of noise which was meant to intimidate and frighten. It was more than simply a noise, it was a declaration that we were facing an army, an army which had declared war on us' : Bernard Jackson, Wath Main picket, *The Battle for Orgreave*

'In a movie I would have thrown down my helmet and shield, stripped off my police tunic and walked away over the horizon ... But this was real life, and, for better or worse, there was no escaping it. It's hard to have ideals in the heat of battle. That ... was the tragedy for everyone who was there who had any connection whatsoever to a mining community' : Mac McLoughlin, from *The English Civil War Part II. Personal Accounts of the 1984–85 Miners' Strike* by Jeremy Deller

Police charge a group of young pickets at Orgreave, 18 June 1984. Note the cavalry in the background. P J Arkell/News Line

EDITOR'S SUMMARY

By 1 June the number of miners arrested exceeded 3,000. Bruce and his small team managed to avoid the roadblocks – and, somewhat remarkably, arrest, despite increasingly frequent police encounters. Nottinghamshire pits continued to be the priority for the early morning excursions, with a 'fall back' to the Orgreave coking plant as a secondary instruction. After a morning at Welbeck on 6 June Bruce describes an assault against a convoy of Orgreave coke lorries, when spiked potatoes and home-made smoke bombs were used. There was no prospect of a settlement to the dispute, talks between the NCB and NUM breaking down after a few days on 13 June. Tragedy struck again two days later when Joe Green was killed by a lorry when picketing outside Ferrybridge Power Station.

The greatest confrontation between pickets and police took place at Orgreave on Monday, 18 June, the one hundredth day of the strike. A mass assembly of miners from all NUM areas had gathered, faced by a formidable army of police deployed from many counties. The pickets were strategically herded into a field near the plant where they were able to be flanked by the police on all sides bar the south where the Sheffield-Worksop railway formed a barrier. Good humour prevailed to begin with, some of the pickets playing football, but the tension increased along with the build up of pickets and police forces, commanded by Assistant Chief Constable Tony Clement. A cordon of long-shielded police were placed in front of the police 'troops'. The usual 'push' forward by the pickets took place when the convoy of lorries arrived. The most dramatic scenes took place when the long-shielded police parted, creating a gap for their mounted colleagues to charge through. Police short-shield squads and police dogs were also used to pursue and disperse the relatively disorganised miners. Some pickets fled in the direction of the railway, having to scramble down the embankment and across the rails whilst others made for the railway bridge. Eventually the miners were forced into the village where charges and stone throwing continued through the streets. Further 'cavalry' charges dispersed the remaining pickets, though some did try to counter this by building barricades. Bruce and his crew managed to escape arrest or injury and he was able to describe aspects of the Orgreave events at first-hand, an experience he likened to a scene from the film, *Spartacus*. Bruce recognised himself on the evening television news footage which included several sequences shown out of order, therefore favouring the police's actions on the day. Jeremy Deller's remarkable re-enactment, staged by Artangel and Event Plan in 2001, was a recreation of most of the actual events, resulting in a film directed by Mike Figgis for Channel 4 television.

Recovering from the Orgreave battle, Bruce and his team continued their picketing of Nottinghamshire pits, a light-hearted and unforgettable moment taking place on the 26th when 'Captain' Bob gained a soaking and lost his cap in a stream, a situation that made him a worthy recipient of the Deed of the Day medal.

THE DIARY
Friday, 1 June

Orders for today – Calverton, Nottinghamshire. Nearly got there but was pressed for time and had to get back to Orgreave. We slowed down a bit today. When the lorries went out we decided not to join the big push and the chanting etc which may have been a good job since several of the lads were injured, one suffering a fractured skull. It was much quieter in the afternoon. We were lucky today not to get injured.

'Opposite forces' assemble and face each other in the large field opposite the Orgreave coking plant where the miners had been placed by the police, on a warm morning, 18 June 1984.
Arthur Wakefield

Many pickets were forced to scramble down the railway embankment at Orgreave to escape from police charges which included the use of Alsation dogs. This remarkable and historic scene was captured on film by Arthur Wakefield, the veteran South Kirkby picket, 18 June 1984.
Arthur Wakefield

Realistic scenes from the 2001 re-enactment of the Battle of Orgreave. Brian Elliott

Saturday, 2 June
Set off for Orgreave but found out that the lorries were not turning out today, or on Sunday. Went home early.

Monday, 4 June
Babbington pit, Notts, then fall back to Orgreave. Set off down the M1 and called at Tibshelf services. At the back there is a little country road, all of the pickets know about it but so do the police. As we got through about a hundred police came towards us, they had just arrived to seal the road but we managed to get to the pit. It was fairly quiet but we had a little push when a lamp post went over and one bobby was hurt. Several others went down an embankment. Made our way to Orgreave but it was quiet today which was how we liked it anyway.

Tuesday, 5 June
Cotgrave pit, Notts. Set off about 9.30 am for the afters shift. Police must have known our destination. All the roads were blocked. Those lads that set off earlier than us got through. Back to Baggin for some snap, then to Orgreave but it was quiet again today.

Wednesday, 6 June
Big day today. Orders were for Welbeck Colliery, then fall back to Orgreave, 4 am start. We planned to ambush a convoy of coke lorries. The previous night, Shaun, Daz, Captain Bob, our kid Bob and myself – and a few lads from Treeton – had a scrounge around. We found old tins of paint and potatoes; and also made some smoke bombs. We poured the paint in bread bags and spiked the spuds. I overlaid, woke up with the clock in my hand at 8 am! Got up, picked the lads up and set off direct to Orgreave. Missed the first convoy. Climbed up to the top of our favourite embankment, overlooking the road that came off the Parkway. Checked our stash of 'ammunition', hidden in some bushes. We waited until they came again which happened about 11.30 am, after only 20 minutes. As the convoy came off the Parkway they had to slow down due to a bend in the road. We were in the trees at the top of an embankment, ready for action. We really gave it to them, and their police fucking escort, who were on motorbikes. One of our lads got carried away and fell down the steep embankment. When we ran out of ammunition there was always a few bricks and stones to throw. Some of the police on bikes tried driving up the embankment – one of them toppled over and nearly fell on top of its rider. It was hit and run today. Daz was overtaken by a truncheon following a skirmish with a fallen policeman. We got away as fast as we could, into the village and mingling with the locals. Made our way back to the front line at Orgreave, bottom end. Hadn't been there long when the police charged. One picket who was just sat on a wall was knocked off and broke his arm. As I was running away I overtook Jack Taylor, the Yorkshire NUM President. I said to him 'Come on Jack, they are not taking prisoners today!' The lorries had been more or less stopped under our missile barrage, drivers ducked beneath their steering wheels. When we reached the car we made a point of driving down the Parkway to have a look at the scene of the 'ambush'. The police vehicles, including their transits, had tried to drive up and over the embankment, you could see all the track marks on the grass. We shared the medal today!

Thursday, 7 June
Orgreave again, 7.30 am. Had a little push and there was some 'Zulu' but fairly quiet today.

Friday, 8 June

Went for a drink tonight in the Titanic WMC at Rawmarsh and got talking to 'Chick' (Stuart) Traquair, a Manvers Main miner. He wanted to come picketing, like a lot of others, especially the older end and was incensed as to what he had seen on television, pickets being badly treated by the police. I informed Chick that new recruits would be always welcome.

Sat/Sun 9–10 June

Wife and kids coming home from visiting her mother in London. Her grandad gave her £100. Didn't go out, though some lads did go to Scunthorpe in the afternoon.

Monday, 11 June

Welbeck Colliery, Notts. Set off at 4am but didn't get through. Turned back to Worksop and was followed out of Notts by a police car. Fell back to Cresswell. One little push but very quiet, so made our way home.

Tuesday, 12 June

No Orgreave. Mansfield Colliery this morning. Set off at 10am. Got through OK. At Pleasley there is a little alleyway at the back of some terraced houses. Used this route now many times. Driving down the alley where they hang their washing etc, arrived about 11.30 am. Weather dull and heavy. A fair turn out for South Notts, about 500 of us, although a lot didn't get

Police asking a local (Harworth) householder if they can have permission to stand in her garden, 13 June 1984.

Police at Harworth move quickly to block a snicket that Bruce and his crew had 'sneaked through'. 13 June 1984.

A line of police 'guard' the lower entrance at Harworth colliery and a police dog patrol van moves towards the pit, 13 June 1984.

through. Some of the scabs smile at you as they are escorted in to the pit. We were a full team: myself, Bob Wilson, Bob Taylor, Shaun Bisby and Darren Goulty.

Wednesday, 13 June
Harworth Colliery, Notts. Weather dull and humid. Set off at 10.am Got about a mile and a half from the pit and then had to walk. About 1,000 to 1,500 pickets were there. We had two little pushes. I took some photos. Right bastards the police – one minute they are talking nice to you and the next they pull a picket from the crowd. They did this twice. Didn't like that. Brian Lonsdale started picketing today (underground locomotive driver from Silverwood Colliery). HM's police today came from:

Worcester
Thames
Nottinghamshire
and Hampshire

Friday, 15 June
Set off this morning for Cadley Hill, NCB South Midlands area. £10 petrol money. Got through with no trouble. A big turn out but no bother. Lovely sunny day. There were a lot of pickets

Pickets outside Cadley Hill colliery, 15 June 1984. In this example, the police allowed a small number of NUM pickets to approach and speak to working miners entering the pit yard (as can be seen in the centre of the photograph, by the large tree). This was 'very unusual', according to Bruce.

Police reinforcements start to appear at Cadley Hill. Note the small number of pickets standing by the tree, 15 June 1984.

The extent of police deployment – to deal with a relatively small assembly of pickets – can be appreciated in this photograph, taken at Cadley Hill, by Bruce, on 15 June 1985. Bob Wilson (wearing a string vest) is just in shot on the left of the photograph, and, immediately to his right, is 'Albert', a Treeton NUM official.

turned back as they went down the M1. We had more sense and diverted down the A38 to Burton on Trent, then headed for Swadlincote on the A444. Police used different tactics today. Stopped all the scabs at the pit gate and let NUM pickets talk to them. They even allowed NUM men on to the coaches. Maybe it's a plan as they don't care about the Staffordshire and Midlands pits. It's the Notts coalfield they want to keep open.

Monday, 18 June
The **Battle of Orgreave.**
Met in the Baggin the previous evening. Something major seems to be happening today. We met in the car park at Treeton/Catcliffe WMC, early morning and it was bright and sunny. When we arrived there were hundreds of cars and vans, a few miners even had 'walkie talkies'. There must have been several thousand of us there. We were instructed to keep quiet, and follow certain people. A Welsh miner reckons we are all hand-picked from local pits. We were to sneak round the the back of the Orgreave plant, reaching Orgreave from the bottom end of the lane. We got in but about 50 police confronted us, then another hundred appeared, some with dogs. A good number of us moved forward to meet them but two-thirds of the pickets hung back. The police tried to take the embankment we were on but we defended with the only weapons we could find – stones and bits of bricks – against shields and truncheons. When they got too close they got dust, we threw dust in their faces which got into their visors, so we managed to repel them down the embankment. They charged at us again wielding truncheons. Paul Burke, a Silverwood lad, came all geared up, wearing a crash helmet and carrying a stick. He launched himself into the police but got nicked. Must be his 4th or 5th arrest. We then marched down to the *Plough* pub, then up towards Orgreave top lane. Met a police roadblock at the slip road into the Sheffield Parkway but managed to break through. Marched up the road within about 600 yards of the other pickets assembled at the top gates but came to another line of police, including horses. That was it, no cavalry coming down here today. Pickets started dismantling a stone wall near the causeway, placing large boulders in the road to create a barrier. Suddenly, a convoy of about fifteen police vans came towards us but had to slow down due to our road obstacles. They were from the bottom end and were bound for their mates at the top. A high-ranking police officer was following them. As the first of the police vans tried negotiating our obstacle course it got greeted with stones, had to swerve and reversed quickly, then forward, smoke coming from the tyres but it did get through – no glass left in the windows though. The man with the 'pips' tried, in a brand new 'A' – reg white car. He failed and was surrounded by pickets, all his windows put through. One lad stood on the roof of his vehicle and dropped a rock through the windscreen, landing it on his lap, and the police officer wrapped his hands around it. He set off back, bouncing off a few boulders, probably writing off the car in the process. We got away fast as the cavalry appeared, coming to the rescue of their commanding officer. The horses didn't get far, due to the obstacles, then an ambulance came. Someone warned the pickets not to move the boulders as the police would get through but some lads did clear a way. The police took advantage and the cavalry charged through, followed by the riot squad. They chased us all the way down to the road on the Parkway. We saw 8 riot police capture a picket, wrapping the lad's hands behind his back, then they started thumping him as they marched with him back up the road. They were also laughing. We shouted 'DON'T LAUGH YOU BASTARDS' and they just blew kisses at us. In one of the police charges, after they had broken through, I was running along with

Scenes of desolation in the streets of Orgreave, 18 June 1984. Arthur Wakefield

an old miner who had to stop and sit down, he was knackered. I just couldn't leave him there so I said to him, 'Come on mi'owd, don't stop, the're not taking any prisoners today', and he got up with difficulty and we both managed to get away but the police continued chasing me. I got well into the fields when a crowd from a factory started cheering me, shouting 'GO ON MATE' and 'COME UP HERE IF YOU CAN.' But managed to escape. The police had their full kit on so were not as fast as me and it was warm.

Made my way back to the bulk of the miners and someone told me that the police were harming pickets brought to Rotherham police station. Went to the *Plough* and met the rest of the team. We had all gone our own ways but everyone was OK. Captain Bob decided that we should go in the pub for a drink. It was a lovely afternoon but we had no money, so we emptied our pockets and managed to scrape together enough change to buy one pint of beer. We sat around a table, all five of us, and passed the pint around, each of us drinking a mouthful. After half an hour we returned to the front line.

This morning, after breaking through the first police line, we came across a lorry parked at the side of the road, but no driver present. It was loaded with hessian sacks containing sand. Was this a coincidence? This morning the worst fighting and violence that I have experienced and seen took place, even by Orgreave standards. At the end of the day I took a cautious walk up to the top of Orgreave, towards the truck place. A right mess – roads blockaded. As I reached the top the cavalry were still around so me and a mate went into the entrance between the terraced houses when a police horse and rider appeared. The copper leaned and peered into the entrance, stick in his hand, and shouted 'COME ON LADS, LET'S HAVE YOU OUT OF THERE.' I told the other miner to stay put as I just did not trust him but he came out of the entrance as instructed. Next minute, I heard a great crack and the picket was holding on to his head and went down on the floor. I went out the back way, through the back gardens of the houses and made my way back. Everything was clear now, you could see what was going on, so I had a good look at what had become a battleground. There was rubble and debris everywhere. Stakes of wood protruded from some piles of rubble, like a scene from the film *Sparticus*. Just the same we had had a good day.

A small bloke wearing a white short-sleeved shirt and sporting an Errol Flynn 'tash came up to me and started chatting, saying, 'You have lost all sympathy from South Yorkshire people today'. Very wary, I just nodded and carried on looking at the battlefield. I could see all the media with cameras on the brow but did not realise at the time that the man who had spoken to me was the 'enemy commander', Assistant Chief Constable Anthony Clement.

Made my way back to the bottom end where I stopped and had a conversation with a group of miners but noticed that police were all over the place, so made my way back through fields and on to the road, keeping out of the way of the bobbies, but I bumped into the riot squad, so went back into the fields again. It was the end of a mighty battle. At the bottom of Orgreave both sides were recuperating, licking their wounds. Got back to the lads and to my car. My mates were there waiting for me, and were surprised when I appeared as they thought I was a gonner. What a day! Everbody back safe, none of us arrested or injured – amazing.

Later that evening I saw myself on TV, near Assistant Chief Constable Clement, surveying the battleground.

Tuesday, 19 June
Newstead Colliery, Notts. £8 petrol money. It's an old pit, not far from Annesley Colliery. It's a nice little place, a very old mine, complete with pit village with old brick terraced houses and

Darren Goulty adjusts his shirt and smiles towards Bruce when on picket duty at Newstead colliery, 19 June 1984. The police officer in charge, from Welwyn Garden City, stands, hands on hip, opposite an NCB coal lorry. More pickets can be seen in the background, some sitting on the grass.

a wooden hut, NUM hut at the pit entrance. Started off quiet today, hot as well. The bobby in charge, a pleasant fellow from Welwyn Garden City, Herts. We sometimes get a decent officer who just wants a quiet life. Coal lorries were going in and out of the pit all day, not a care in the world. With Daz, 'Commander Bond' and Shaun we went into the woods for ammo but dashed out when an NCB bus, a legitimate target, appeared. We waved but had missed him.

Darren Goulty (right foreground) is being approached by a senior police officer at Cresswell Colliery, Derbyshire, 20 June 1984.

Another scene at Creswell colliery, 20 June 1984. Police in light-coloured jackets were regarded as the 'snatch squad' by the pickets.

Returned to the woods, dashed out and threw stuff towards a lorry which stopped and parked up, the driver needing medical assistance.

Wednesday, 20 June
Set off for South Notts but couldn't get through, so fell back to Cresswell and that took some getting to. There were coppers all over when we got there. Gave them the run around. One chased me. He shouted, 'EH, GODFREY, DON'T GO DOWN THERE!' I replied, 'Why not?' He jumped over a wall for me. I did not run, just stood still and looked at him. He calmed down and told me to stop fucking about and get back to the rest of the pickets which I did. Lucky Bruce! faced with the picket line, two scabs turned round and went home.

Thursday, 21 June
On days. Bentinck. 4 am start. £6 petrol money but overlaid.

Friday, 22 June
Days. Bevercotes. 4 am start. £6 petrol money. Overlaid again.

Monday, 25 June
Newstead, South Notts. £8 petrol money. Played cat and mouse with roadblocks. Didn't get stopped, just ran through them. Sneaked through at Pleasley. Shaun and Daz sat playing *All*

A policeman shares a joke with three pickets at Newstead, Notts, 25 June 1984.

Bleeding Hearts in the tea hut. Myself and rest of crew on the front line, shouting 'YOU SCABBING BASTARDS!' Bob Wilson was threatened with arrest, so he pretended to jump out at two passing scabs and coppers nearly had a heart attack. While we were waiting for the scabs to arrive Barney Kilgallen came marching down, flask in hand and everyone shouted 'SCAB' but, Barney, a Silverwood lad, was not a scab but a picket!

Tuesday, 26 June
A day out into Nottinghamshire, when Captain Bob lost his flat cap

Orders for today – head for Notts. Managed to get to Pleasley. Saw the road block ahead, just a lone policeman on a little bridge over a stream. Stopped our battlebus out of sight of the policeman and let the commandos out. I drove on but was waved down by the bobby. 'Morning Sir, what is your name and where are you bound?' I told him my name, using my best southern-type accent and said that I was visiting my grandmother who lives in Pleasley. 'OK, Sir' and he waived me on! I drove a short distance until out of his sight, parked up and waited for my commandos. I stood looking at a spot where the stream narrowed. I saw my mates coming out of the bushes twenty-five yards away. Bob Wilson jumped across the stream, then Daz, followed by Shaun. All of them made it, without any problem. Then it was Captain Bob's turn. Being a big lad, Bob landed in the middle of the water and started cursing as he was wet through. He crawled out, hauling himself on to the bank, soaked to the bone, builders' arse showing as well. All we could hear from him was 'Were's mi cap? Mi cap's gone! Mi fucking

Bob Wilson adjusts his camera whilst, in the background 'Captain' Bob Taylor searches for his lost cap, following his unexpected swim in a Pleasley stream.

Like two explorers, Bob and Darren try and recover from their aquatic experience in wild and wet Derbyshire.

cap! It's gone, mi cap!' We went searching for the said cap but it's probably in the North Sea by now. We looked downstream and searched high and low. Bob loved that cap, especially since he is thinning a bit on top. He kept talking about his lost cap all the way home. In fact we had never seen him without his cap. He will have to save up his picket money for a new one. Had enough today. Beat the roadblock, just the one but I don't think we were in a fit state to picket. Owd Bob's cap gave us a big laugh, though. We think he went to bed in it. He was game for a laugh, though. We dropped him off at Rawmarsh Baths, but he had a fair walk to get home, all wet through. You ought to have seen him: all he had on was an old pair of blue bri-nylon underpants, an old child's Winnie the Pooh duffle coat which I found in the car boot – so small that it only came to his crotch. It's a good job he wasn't spotted by the police as he could have been arrested. Captain Bob won the Deed of the Day medal for the entire week.

Wednesday, 27 June

Rufford Colliery, nr Mansfield. £8 petrol money. Set off this morning but couldn't get through. Used all the usual shortcuts but the roads were all blocked. Returned to Silverwood Welfare and had a bite to eat. After picketing, somedays me and the wife and kids went to Swinton Civic Centre where we could have a free dinner, which was served all week, Monday to Friday. At Silverwood we could also get a dinner and a food parcel once a week, and from the Dalton & Sunnyside Community Centre we could get a carrier bag full of goodies – a bag of sugar, couple of tins of beans, teabags, margarine, tin of peaches, jar of jam. Good job that the kids like jam – we have a cupboard full. That night went for a pint with my dad, to the *Alpine*, at Rockingham. He always bought me a couple of pints on his pay day. He's a redundant steelworker. It was crowded inside. Dad's mate, who was well merry, asked me if I was a striking miner. I told him that I was and he left to go somewhere. Twenty minutes later he returned, with a carrier bag full of food – there was an opened box of cornflakes, half a bag of sugar, a big handful of teabags – and a full jar of jam. His heart was certainly in the right place. I remember one old miner having his free meal in Silverwood Miners' Welfare when he put his reading glasses on. His mate asked him what he was doing wearing his glasses and he told him that it made his dinner looked bigger.

Thursday, 28 June

Rufford Colliery, near Mansfield. £8 petrol money. Set off at 9.30am from Baggin. Same route, through Whiston crossroads to Clowne, but roadblocks were all over. Still not impossible to get through, though. All the side roads off the main Worksop road were sealed. Drove back and forward for a while, made our way to Worksop and came to a roadblock – turned back, all the lads in the back giving the coppers some lip and making rude gestures. One copper at roadblock waved his wallet. Finished up on a roundabout near the motorway. Stopped yet again but argued with the policeman that we should not be stopped in Derbyshire. He waved to a motorbike bobby who told us to follow him and he would show us the way home. He led us and Brian Lonsdale's car to the motorway. As he turned off the roundabout for the M1 we kept going round, Brian following did the same. You should have seen the police! Their arms were waving all over the place. Next time we came to a motorway exit, we obliged them and we could hear them shout 'GET THAT CAR!' Anyway, went south on motorway and came off at the first exit but we were stopped again. A copper walked in front of the car – nearly ran over his toes. As I set off he was leaning on the bonnet. He warned me that for driving like this he would arrest me next time he saw me. Same again, another roundabout, signalled to go left but kept going round and the coppers going into the road waving and panicking. Got on the M1 again and went north this time. Copper asked Brian 'Which way did that brown Triumph go' and Brian said 'South'. Ha Ha! Back down into Derbyshire, through Kiveton etc and finished up on the same bit of main road that we had started on. Shaun, Bob and Daz gave police at roadblocks some abuse. Next thing I know, looking in my mirror, there were two transits full of police following us. One overtook us and then I overtook him – or tried to. He crushed me to the side of the road. Had to stop as there was a van full of them behind us as well managed to get away just as they both pulled up, we shot off, not speeding but I kept putting my right indicator on as if to turn right, stopping them overtaking me. Played cat and mouse for about a mile when, suddenly, the road widened. That was it. I did what I could and pulled up in a public place where people could see what was going on. The coppers surrounded us. I switched the engine off and was told to get out of the car. They meant business these lads. They searched the car, emptied the boot, even threw back seats into a field, we'd really got to them. A big copper told Shaun he was going to take him in the field and knock the stuffing out of him, and the same with the others. Shaun said something to the big copper and the copper then threatened to push his head in the radiator and switch the fan on. He told Shaun that no one calls him a wanker. It was a very, very lucky escape for us today. Thought we were all definitely nicked. The police sergeant told his mates to note my car reg number. Anyway, it was only 11 am, so we tried our luck for Cresswell, getting there a few minutes later. Had a walk around, all was quiet, then set off home, back to Silverwood Welfare for some snap.

Friday, 29 June
Mansfield Colliery. £8 petrol money. Set off from Silverwood Miners' Welfare at 9.40 am. Tried a different way – down Sheffield Parkway, then took the Chesterfield route, down the dual carriageway to the motorway but about a mile from Pleasley it was swarming with police. Sent back up the M1 northwards but came off at Cresswell and followed a big lorry off the motorway. Lads in the back of the car crouched down and kept close to the lorry, driving past one roundabout and then another but at a third a copper walked into the road and flagged me down. I paused to slow down, then carried on. You should have seen his face! Hoped that I wouldn't bump into him again. We carried on and nobody followed us, getting all the way to Pleasley, then Glapwell and towards Hardwick Hall and country lanes but reached another roadblock. A policeman was talking to pickets in a car when us and three other cars with pickets on board drove passed him, without stopping. 'SOD HIM!' all the lads shouted some abuse as we went by but it was a good job that Shaun was not with us today – the policeman would have used his radio, and sent someone chasing after us. Managed to get to Mansfield at about 11.25 am. Only us and another car from Silverwood were there to begin with. Only been there a few minutes when Bob shouts out 'SCAB!' and was warned that he would be arrested. One worker threw his cap into the pickets and went home. We all cheered. Earlier, a policemen fell down an embankment and we all laughed. One picket, just walking to join us, was then nicked, just to save policeman's face? Bob was warned again by a senior officer for making comments to a policeman who had broken wind, very loudly, making a right stink and blaming it on 'northern beer'. A fairly quiet day. Returned to Baggin, last back again.

IV
$\mathcal{P}its,\ \mathcal{P}ower\ \mathcal{S}tations\ and\ a$ $\mathcal{P}olice\ \mathcal{C}ell\ in\ \mathcal{S}cunthorpe$
July 1984

'They offered us stew and chips, …
and we heard Spartacus in the next cell!'

Pickets 'taking control' of traffic at the Selby toll bridge in July 1984.

EDITOR'S SUMMARY

There was no let up in strike activities for our Silverwood pickets during July and by the end of the month their luck had run out, joining a burgeoning list of over 4,000 arrested miners. On 5 July the NUM met the NCB for a series of talks which collapsed thirteen days later – chiefly concerning interpretations of the term 'uneconomic' in relation to the life of pits. Most of the crew's picketing took place in the Nottinghamshire heartland, notably at Pye Hill colliery, where, on 10 July, they found themselves in a perfect situation to attack a coach load of scabs. However, the working miners were not only able to exit their bus but give chase to Bruce and his crew, an unforgettable experience for each of them. It was towards the end of the month, on 24 July, that they found themselves confined for a few hours in a Scunthorpe cell, following an expedition to picket Gunness Wharf where Polish coal was being unloaded. The local police treated them very well and the bail conditions did nothing to deter them from further picketing activities, since they were chased by a police transit van the following day at Pleasley, escaping via a disused railway track. Bruce's battlebus or Triumph 2.5 saloon continued to serve them well despite a failed MOT on 16 July. A letter asking for the NUM to assist in the small problem of repairs, road tax and insurance – and also stating their picketing prowess – not only had the desired effect but resulted in exceptional hilarity amongst the local NUM strike committee.

THE DIARY
Monday, 2 July

Got our orders and my £7 petrol money, off to Selby today. Set off at 4 am. Arrived at Whitemoor pit, Selby Complex, 5.30 am. Didn't know at the time but it was picket contractors who came at 8 am, so there was a mix up somewhere. A cold morning, raining. Nothing going on, so about thirty of us went to the plant, at the back, where the scabs would come in. Police sent marching squads to intercept us; then the convoy arrived. We gave it some 'Ooh! Ooh!' and 'Zulu'. I got lifted off my feet due to the squeezing and shoving. Didn't have much choice about it. There was a load of pickets behind me. I finished up in a six-foot deep ditch, with mud in the bottom. Four coppers went in as well! Everyone of us came out wet and sludgy. One picket dragged Andy Summat (?) out. He sat on the bank and didn't have a clue where he was. We were sludged up to the eyeballs and soaked to the skin. Another lad, Mick Reid's brother, was pulled out, sludged up the bollacks, he wasn't pleased. When we got in to the plant 'Captain Sensible' Lee started dishing sticks out to fight the coppers off. The police were OK, though – West Yorkshire bobbies. Four lads picked me up and used me as a barricade! 'Captain Sensible' Lee picked Shaun up and charged through the police – Lee was a big lad! They broke right through the police line. After a good day out there were no casualties. Went back to the car. On the way back some idiot drove up close to a milk float and lifted a bottle of pop. A woman witnessed it and informed the milk float driver who went up to the miner's car and threatened to call the police, so they gave the pop back. Good job that they did as you can get arrested for nothing now, so nicking bottle of pop would mean a life sentence. All quiet on the Western Front!

Tuesday, 3 July

Did the impossible today – got to Clipstone. Met a nice policeman today. £8 petrol money.

Set off from Silverwood Miners' Welfare. Brian Lonsdale followed us. Made the mistake of going through Pleasley. Hardwick Hall sign at Glapwell, just in the dip before entering

Mansfield, there was a police car hidden in the hedge 'picket spotting'. We got half a mile up the road when he pulled out and followed us, siren going at first to let us know he was after us. He overtook Brian who only had Tommy with him in his car. He stopped behind us. I stopped in the middle of the road so that he could not pull in front of us but after a bit I thought it would be wise if I pulled over a bit, so I moved over and waved Brian on. Police pulled me and took my name and address. I was instructed to turn around in no uncertain terms. They can swear when they want can those police. I turned round a corner, then put my foot down, dodging and weaving cars and a heavy lorry, frightening my commandos to death; then up and down country lanes. After hitting a farmer's gatepost, moving it a couple of feet, manoeuvred into the farmyard, stopped and parked next to a low wall next to the road. Two minutes later 'jam sandwich' came by slowly. He looked over the wall. We were caught again! Farmer started moaning about compensation. Shaun, Daz and Bob sat with the police while one copper told me to get in the car and took my details. I sat in the passenger seat with one foot in the car and the other on the road, the car door open. The policeman told me that they were not all bastards like my mates seem to think. I went along with him. He told me that his dad was a striking Nottinghamshire miner and that he could do me for reckless driving etc etc; but he also said that I had enough on my plate without having to face fines, so just gave me a producing ticket – but also warned me that if I was seen anywhere in Notts again that day I would be arrested. So, we set off again for an unknown destination. Finished up on the Ollerton Road, the lads ducked down in the car as usual and we managed to get through two roadblocks. At the first one the coppers were changing over shifts and at the second they were 'laxydaisy' and we got through to Clipstone Colliery, near Mansfield. The police were very surprised to see us as it was just about impossible to get through by car, the only other way would have been on foot or on a bus. Parked outside the pit and got out of the car, ideal position for picketing. Canteen on the main road was full of scabs! Cars and buses pulling up outside the pit entrance full of scabs. Twenty minutes later a police patrol car drove past my car and had a good look. They were from one of the Mansfield area roadblocks. I knew we were marked men as soon as I got back in the car after the farmhouse incident. Got back in the car and only moved a few feet when a police Landrover pulled out into the road a few yards in front of me. Thinking my number was up, I put a crooklock on my steering wheel, and locked the car, as I did not think I would be using it for a while. Started walking back to the pickets when a copper called me over but I stayed put but have a pause decided to slowly make my way towards him. I was in no hurry to get nicked. Two more bobbies converged on me, one of the more high ranking than the other, and built like a brick toilet. I looked in awe. He looked like he had a cardboard box under his tunic. I asked him if his shoulders were real or padded. Their No.1 said to me, 'Listen, son, a friendly bit of advice. You've been warned twice today. You've had a bloody good run. One to you for getting through, but today's today and tomorrow's another day. So if you come back tomorrow you are nicked, son.' I joined the rest of the lads. I have nothing but respect for those striking Notts miners. We stood and picketed with the handful that were there.

End of shift, went back to the strike centre and had a cup of tea. It was a big wooden hut. Felt sorry for them, main meal of the day was salad. All the Notts strikers and their families were in this wooden building. They were having a very rough time, arrested for just saying 'Boo!'. The police are intimidating them badly. I think they got a boost by us being there as they had been on their own for some time. Earlier on, walking by the pit canteen, I waited for a scab to have the guts to look up from his tea when I did not half lace into him – verbally. Sup that tea and enjoy it, mate, I thought, as next week there will be 3,000 of us coming down. They knew they were in the wrong because they did not look us in the face, even when there were dozens of them and just ten of us – they looked down at the floor, anywhere but at us.

Wednesday, 4 July
Pye Hill. £8 petrol money. There must be 180 pits in England and we keep being sent here! Went down the Sheffield Parkway, then on to Chesterfield and got through OK. On the picket line a policeman asked me if I had any trouble with the overdrive on my Triumph 2.5 (battlebus to us) car. I had a chat with him and told him that I had no trouble as my overdrive did not work. He was nice and polite, then the scabs arrived so I said 'Excuse me, I must dash'. Just goes to show, they don't miss anything. After the scabs went in things were quiet so got talking to a London bobby. He was a young lad, just like us, and he asked us what the strike was all about. Also, what sort of trouble took place. We wasted no time in getting our case across, then the police gaffer came over and instructed us to get back to our places. Can't believe the young bobby didn't know what the strike was about!

Made our way back home but on a country lane my car exhaust dropped off, making a right noise, scraping on the road surface. Several other picket cars stopped and checked to see if we were OK. I went into the boot and took a hammer out. As I was laid under the car, banging away, a police car pulled up, about twenty foot away, a bobby and a women officer inside. I got up to have a look, not realising that I had a hammer in my hand. They shouted to me to put the hammer down. I started walking towards them in order to explain what I was doing, even pointing to the hammer and then the car but as I got closer the bobby put his car into reverse and shifted fast – he thought that I was about to attack him! A good job that there were plenty of pickets and not just the two police. Bet I would have been charged – but what with? Wonder what tales their commanding officer had been telling them for bedtime stories about miners!

Thursday, 5 July
£8 petrol money. Pye Hill. Pot luck getting there, it's a waste of time anyway. Lads got down in the back of the car at Junction 27 of the M1. I did not slow down. When we got through the lads got up and gave the coppers a wave, which left them scratching their heads. Mind you, though, they let so many through to find out where everyone was heading. Silly me, took a wrong turning, drove by Annesley, Linby and Newstead collieries into Mansfield. We came to a road block, manned by the Met! We were stopped and turned around, so had to go back later to the same roadblock; coppers stopping us again. They wanted to know who'd been calling them 'wankers' with hand signals but nobody owned up. A copper said it was that lad in the back – Shaun had been at it again! We were let go with a warning. As we set off found out that we were going the wrong away again, so we turned round and went back. Same roadblock yet again. We waved to them as we went passed, told them we had had enough and that we were going sunbathing instead. Finally, made it to Pye Hill Colliery. Penned in again. Shaun, Darren and myself had a walk around the village, it keeps coppers on their toes but no luck as we got turned back at the road to the pit entrance. Went back to the rest of the pickets. After ten minutes we were bored. Tried our luck again, under hedges, over fields, climbed up an old slag heap, overgrown with trees. A copper saw us and sent one of his men to get us. We saw him getting closer, then he shouted 'NOW THEN, COME HERE YOU BASTARDS!' He took

Picket Shaun Bisby at Pye Hill (Notts) on 5 July 1984, the policeman reluctant to be identified on film.

his hat off and wiped his forehead. Mind you, he was OK. 'Testing your defences', I said to the copper. On the way back Shaun stood next to a copper. I told him to stay there so that I could take a picture but the copper would not have it, turned and walked away but still took a photograph. Generally quiet today, although after setting off, a coach load full of workers tried to get through, so all the pickets drove their cars into the middle of the road. The coach got through by driving partly on the causeway. We all went home and had a cup of tea at the Baggin.

Heard on the grapevine that there was a free do for striking miners at Sheffield City Hall. Told the wife. Got Shaun and his Mrs and we set off for the free dinner and dance. We met Shaun and his Mrs in Rotherham and set off, hoping to hitch it because of shortage of money. Gay put her thumb up and a car stopped straight away. When we arrived at the Sheffield City Hall there weren't many people there. We were too early. We were given free beer tickets at the door but no buffet. We came away early, no money, just enough for a taxi to get us to Rotherham but our money ran out on the meter at Templeborough so we had to walk, but managed to get another lift almost straight away. Dropped Shaun and his wife off at

Rotherham, and me and Gay got taken all the way to Rawmarsh, the lad was glad to help us out, hearing we were miners.

Friday, 6 July

Selby. £7 petrol money. Meet at Silverwood Miners' Welfare, as usual, 6.30 am, destination Whitemoor pit, part of the Selby complex. Weather cloudy and drizzly. When we arrived there was a mass picket on! Running battles all day, just like old times at Orgreave. We climbed over hills to get to the rest of the pickets. There was a bit of pushing and shoving when we got there, police pushing some pickets into a field. A large group of us decided to walk back up the road, so we climbed over a fence, out of our 'pen'. Pickets were arriving from all over, to build numbers up; then somebody tipped a police transit van on its side. Seeing this, coppers charged up the road and everybody scattered, the riot police followed up. Coppers chased one bloke down the road and instead of arresting him when the caught him they threw him into a ditch. The riot squad chased us to the top of a hill but they got a right hammering. You could not see the sky for missiles, and a couple of them went down. Missiles were thrown that thick and fast that the police couldn't mover forward. A couple more of them went down and we retreated again (got a picture of it). Some pickets sneaked around the back of the police and put a transit in a ditch.

Running battles again. Could see and hear a mass of pickets giving it some 'Zulu' down the road. Pickets were falling into ditches and there were clouds of dust everywhere. North

Pickets on rough ground near Whitemoor colliery (Selby complex), 6 July 1984. Bruce and his fellow pickets were warned by a police officer to 'move away' or dogs would be set on them. A few minutes later riot police attacked the group from the left side of this scene.

A composite picture reminiscent of a scene on the Somme rather that 1980s Yorkshire. This sequence shows pickets charged away by a 'troop' of riot police at Whitemoor on 6 July 1984, some pickets able to view the action from the relative safety of the roadside verges. Bob Taylor

Yorkshire police and London police were there, never seen badges like theirs before. Things quietened down. Me and the lads went back to the rest of the pickets on the road. One lad came up to me and asked to swop shirts as he had been involved in some kind of 'dirty deed' but had been spotted by the police, so was a marked man, so we agreed to swop. Police were mingling with pickets but we kept quiet. Six coaches of police reinforcements came through, so off we went, trekking over the hills again. Tried to get to the road where the scabs (contractors) went down. Two policemen with dogs came up to us. They told us to clear off up the hill or they would release their dogs on us! One lad carrying a stick was told to drop it or the dog would go for him. Poor lad had to do as he was told. Took a photo of a copper and his dog.

Police in riot squad gear arrive by special bus, to aid other uniformed officers at Whitemoor, 6 July 1984.

A police officer and dog approach a small number of pickets who were attempting to reach Whitemoor pit ' by the back door'. Note the stone, held in the left hand of the man in the foreground, in case the dog attacked, 6 July 1984.

An eventful day. Everyone went home but on the way back stopped next to a field and picked some lettuces. Mind you, couldn't get back through Selby as there were a thousand pickets blocking off the town and a contractor's van had been turned over a bridge. The contractors stayed inside their upturned vehicle with their pickax handles. There was a fifteen mile tailback of traffic. Police couldn't get through, there was all hell let loose but no violence or wrecking. We detoured to go down the A1. The six police coaches were late getting through. Our lads had blockaded a bridge, forcing them to come the long way round.

Sunday, 8 July

MacGregor and Scargill talking for nine hours last Thursday (5 July), talks resumed on Friday for another five hours, then they were to meet again tomorrow, 9 July. I think it is the same old story, build you up and drop you down, hoping the men would get fed up and start drifting back to work. Last week Thatcher and the NCB started a major propaganda programme. Bet these talks are all part of this strategy. Might get power cuts in the autumn.

End of autumn army on red alert to shift coal stocks, the Government burning oil to save coal stocks ... nuclear power stations run minus safety overhauls etc. In today's *News of the World* MacGregor's Plan for Coal is virtually the same as they have been saying for the last four months:

A letter written by Bruce – from the viewpoint of picket – is published in the Rotherham Advertiser *on 7 July 1984.*

Run down of pits in two years.
Heavy investment in new superpits .
Definition of what the term 'uneconomic' means.

Can't see Arthur agreeing to these – between the lines it says the same as before!

I've heard that Ogreave might be opening up tomorrow.

Monday, 9 July

Pye Hill again. £8 petrol money. Set off on the old route: Chesterfield, Alfreton, A1 etc, getting to Pye Hill at 11 am. Pickets stood watching as usual. We sneaked around the back, dodging the police, going through hedges etc and got to the pit gates. Started talking to a young copper who was on duty. Daz sneaked up on him, crawling through the grass, commando-style, holding a small branch in the air, placed in front of face for camouflage. Copper wondered what on earth was happening. Me and Shaun were pissing ourselves with laughter, hiding in the trees. For the young copper, it was his first day on picket duty. He came from Wembley. Had a natter with another London copper. Couldn't believe it – he let us stop and picket but we got fed up after half an hour and returned with the rest of the lads.

Had a game of cards in the pub and listened to the pickets 'Boo' the coaches full of scabs, then made our way back to Silverwood Miners' Welfare. Heard that 'Talks had broken out', looks like settling the dispute but MacGregor refused to sign at the last minute. They are meeting again on 18 July, a Wednesday, on the same day that I go to court for non-payment of fines. When I got home they had come and taken our telly away. Went an ordered a slot-meter telly which takes 50p pieces.

One lad at Silverwood has a young 'un about five years old, he was paying £1 electric but YEB changed their policy and told him he will have to pay £7.50 a week and he's got a bill for £82. They are going to cut his electricity supply on Thursday.

Heard that Orgreave is opening up today.

Tuesday, 10 July
Pye Hill again. Back down to Chesterfield, to the A61, Alfreton, turn off at Somercotes and Selston signs. The scabs go down at Underwood. Two shafts at Pye Hill – No 1 & No 2. Busy day today, not too many pickets, me, Darren, Capt Bob and Shaun had a look around and Captain Bob got a film for his camera today!

Where the road form a 'V', off the motorway and Mansfield Road, we sat on the grass verge. 'Top Bobby' drove passed us and waved! He likes a quiet life for himself and his troops but we're getting bored. We'd been talking to the same police superintendent the day before. I'm sure we told him that we were from Silverwood. He's not daft – probably knew what we had had for our suppers last night! At 12.10 pm our signaller gave us the sign that a coach was on its way. Daz stood on the opposite side of the road. Captain Bob, Shaun and myself sat on a bench by the bus stop. The bus driver thought we were scabs! He pulled into the bus bay and I walked in front of him and, as I heard the hiss of the door opening, I launched a big stone at his windscreen which shattered it. That started it. He got it from all directions. Darren attacked from the other side, Shaun from the back and 'David Bailey' took some pictures.

I started walking away. One picket waved two fingers, shouting, 'SCABBING BASTARDS!' and another two shouted something similar. That did it. Some scabs on the bus stood up, shouting at their police escort 'WHAT ARE GOING TO DO ABOUT THAT? YOU ARE SUPPOSED TO PROTECT US.' I don't know if anyone got hurt but didn't wait to find out as the scabs went wild, piled off the bus and gave chase. As we ran we heard them shout, 'GET THAT FAT BASTARD', meaning poor old Bob Taylor, but we couldn't help each other. it was every man for himself. We really got to them today. We missed a snicket and ran up someone's driveway. A dog came out. We just managed to get over a fence to shouts of 'WE'LL HAVE YOU BASTARDS' and get back to the rest of the pickets. Couldn't see Bob Taylor. Maybe he got caught and thumped. The scabs were in a killing mood. I took my black and red striped teashirt off and gave it to 'Razzer', a Silverwood lad but told him to keep it out of sight and that I would explain later.

Good job that we did not drive straight away as all the cars that did were stopped and checked. A witness from the coach that we attacked was in a police van looking at the pickets. We have to go to the same place tomorrow as well! A lad from a Yorkshire pit, Dean, was being dragged out of a car, wearing the same type of shirt as me!

Coppers were on bridges every 500 yards signalling to each other. Back at the Baggin one lad told me that he saw two squad cars race off towards the buses. One scab waved his snap box at a sergeant and shouted, 'WHERE WERE YOU? YOU WERE SUPPOSED TO PROTECT US'. A lot of men did not go to work that day. On the motorway going home there were police all over the place. A Jaguar patrol car followed us and overtook us twice. We didn't get nicked but maybe our numbers will be up tomorrow.

If we had set off first I can't think what they might have done to us. Back at the picket line we bumped into 'Superintendent Bloggs' – he didn't know what we had done. I think our union officials were pleased with us, breaking the monotony of things. Ah well, one to us. All's fair, they say, in love and war!

Wednesday, 11 July

Pye Hill again. Well, I must say after yesterday we are either brave or stupid. Back to Pye Hill, land of 'Lady Chatterley's Lover'. No wonder that they carry on working here – the road to the pit entrance has posh bungalows on either side. They ought to see where I live in the concrete canyon, pupose-built pit houses from the 1950s.

Turned out to be a good day. Only a handful of us got through. We didn't try too hard. Heard the police were after blood. Three lads nicked already. We may not have tried hard but we did get through. We heard that the three nicked lads were arrested carrying squeezy bottles of pop, classed as offensive weapons.

When we got back to the Baggin Mick Bush said, 'Wilson, you bastard, nobody got through!' I did not realise it at the moment, but I must have set off too early and the police were crafty, letting a few pickets' cars through just to see where they were heading, then closed the roads, so as to concentrate their efforts on one pit.

'Captain' Bob Taylor was always pleased when he was awarded the 'Deed of the Day' medal.

We awarded Captain Bob Taylor our Deed of the Day medal for the rest of the week, it's an old 100 yards swimming medal with NUM stickers on it, complete with a gaudy ribbon. Terry, from Silverwood, told me three months later that the landlord of a local pub gave police the registration numbers of cars parked in his car park. Some Thrybergh lads were dragged out of their beds in the middle of the night and taken to Mansfield police station and were believed to have had seven bells knocked out of them. They knew who was responsible but would not tell. What men!

Thursday, 12 July

Me and Captain Bob went to the Baggin. Our orders for today – Bentinck. Picked all the lads

Pickets, including Shaun Bisby and Bob Wilson, walking to Bentinck, on a quiet day, 12 July 1984.

up and got through OK, straight through to Pleasley. Old Grant got nicked at the pit gates. Quiet.

Friday, 13 July
Orders for today – Linby first, then Warsop. Difficult, but got through. Quiet. Fell back to Warsop. When we arrived the riot police were there, got to be army, too disciplined and six feet tall, must be the Coldstream fucking guards. Battling all morning, wouldn't let us over the bridge but got through, 8.am. Police didn't stand no shit today, wanted it and had it all their own way. Dave got nicked. Some pickets in the back of transits got some fist. Lads dry now. Fell in stream at Pleasley again – what devotion to duty!

Monday, 16 July
Destination Rufford power station. £10 petrol money. Radcliffe on Soar. Unintentionally we led a convoy of about fifteen cars from Silverwood to about five miles from the power station. Nothing doing. London coppers. We just stood in a field.

My battlebus failed its test! Before the test ran out the union paid my insurance for 12 months (£57) and car tax (£50). In order to get funding I had to write a letter to the NUM Branch Secretary, stating what the problem was, cost of repair and so on. My letter went something like this:

> *Dear Sirs,*
> *My name is Bruce Wilson. My car Registration number..........has failed its*
> *test. I have had a quote of £100 for repairs, plus road tax of £50, and*
> *insurance of £57 for twelve months.*
> *I would hope the NUM would consider my case for funding.*
> *There's five of us who go out picketing every day. Granville Richardson*
> *will verify all details. If I go off the road the NUM will lose five good lads,*
> *we want to go on picketing, we earn our picket money and we can, and do,*
> *do some damage. We make the police earn their money.*

Later, Granville pulled me up in the Silverwood Miners' Welfare and told me that my request for funding was granted but when he'd done laughing, he told me that my letter had the meeting of NUM officials in stitches, and for me never to put anything in writing like that again! Point taken, but desperate men take desperate measures. I heard that they voted unanimously to grant me funds.

I didn't believe it at the time but we were classed as one of Arthur's 'hit squads', but we did not know and he certainly didn't.

Tuesday, 17 July
The day's orders – Bentinck. £8 petrol money. Managed to get through. Very quiet. Had to walk into the village, up from the pit. Threw a few stones at coal lorries. Coppers couldn't work out where they were coming from. Missed the windscreens. Back to the Baggin. Cup of tea and summat to eat.

Wednesday, 18 July
Orders – Bentinck Colliery. Had a day off. Talks between MacGregor and Scargill broke down after nine hours.

Thursday, 19 July

Got my picket money. Me and Captain Bob had a day off but Silverwood lads went to (guess!) – Bentinck. Heard later that some Silverwood men came across some scabs on a bend, a blind spot near the pit where nobody could see anything. Six scabs walking to work. The lads got the last one. The other five didn't even turn around, just left their mate on his own. He went moaning to the coppers, saying that he had got smacked.

Friday, 20 July

Set off for Bentinck. Just before Clowne, the roads were blocked. Stopped at one roadblock and my commandos went through some fields. I carried on in the car and waited for them. Got through the roadblock but coppers waved me back. I was stood next to the car, forgetting about the police, looking for the lads. Coppers continued to wave to me but I refused to respond. They then shouted, 'WE WANT A WORD WITH YOU – JUST TO TALK FOR A FEW MINUTES.' Like a fool, I walked over to them and was then immediately apprehended. Just then, my commandos appeared from the bushes. After a protest from my mates, a sergeant told his men to let me go.

Monday, 23 July

Set off from Silverwood Miners' Welfare, early morning, bound for a Notts pit. Couldn't get through so fell back to Cresswell, Derbyshire. Quiet morning, just a bit of shouting at the scabs. Made our way back to base, had a cup of tea and relaxed for half an hour, then dropped the lads off home.

Tuesday, 24 July

The day we got nicked at Gunness Wharf.

Set off at 7.45 am, to Gunness Wharf, Scunthorpe where they were unloading imported coal from Poland. Massive convoys of miners' cars. No chance of getting through. Only three ways to get there and you had to cross a bridge, each way, with coppers all over. Got as far as the

Part of the nine-mile traffic jam on the M180 when Bruce and his mates played football to pass the time – on the day they finished up in a Scunthorpe cell: 24 July 1984.

bridge but they wouldn't let us through. We walked up an embankment with another couple of hundred pickets. Tried getting around their backs but the police held firm. So we made our way back to the main road. The police must have been expecting trouble as they ran to their transits and swopped their noddy hats for riot helmets and then assembled on the road, two deep. We all stopped for a while, then dispersed. That was when Shaun and Daz got chased, bobbies chasing them through a cornfield. When the police caught up with them, one said, 'What shall we nick 'em for?' Another one replied, ' What about damaging a cornfield?' But they managed to get away. Someone shouted, 'ONTO THE MOTORWAY!' whereupon everyone jumped into their cars and made off. We got on the M180 but when we finally got going there were only a handful of cars that made it but suddenly we found ourselves in front of all the traffic, all five of us commandos in one of the leading cars. We got drawn into the situation unintentionally, stuck in the middle lane. All four lanes, including the hard shoulder, came to a slow halt. Lads wasted no time. they jumped out of the car and started to play football. Don't know where the ball came from! After half an hour of talking and discussions on the motorway and football game finished, a coach full of elderly ladies were just behind us, getting fed up. Being respectful and polite I pulled forward and let them out and then reversed back into my gap. Big mistake! The ladies were writing down our registration details! We set

off. I had covered my number plate with old newspapers. A policeman pulled up on the opposite side of the motorway and began taking car numbers as well. My car was easy to spot, a big brown Triumph 2.5 litre, with white alloy wheels.

The newspapers covering my plate did not last long, soon blew away. A police transit van pulled up along the side of us as we were driving down the motorway. I put my foot down but couldn't get far in the traffic. The police transit pulled alongside again. The police occupants did not look very pleased with us, and were dressed in riot gear, black gear and helmets. They signalled for me to pull over. I slowed down and they pulled over about ten yards in front of me. Suddenly the back doors of their

Documentation relating to Bruce Wilson's arrest at Scunthorpe, 24 July 1984 when he was remanded to appear before the Magistrates' Court on 22 August, for 'obstructing the highway.'

94

van was kicked open and they came flying out. Anybody would think that they were the SAS. I did not wait to find out so pulled back onto the motorway and sped off. The police were ever so funny, it was like a scene from the Keystone Cops. When I set off, they ran back to their transit and started pushing each other back into the van. They finally caught up with us again, breaking all speed records in the process. They meant business, so I made a point of pulling off at a junction where public visibility was good, and then slowed down. I noticed a shoe flying out of the car in front me! We didn't argue, just got into the back of the police transit. The floor and seats were covered with 'Girlie' mags. Our kid (Bob) said 'So this is what you spend your wages on, and what you read while waiting for us'. We were told to shut up in no uncertain terms and taken to Scunthorpe police station's nick. Glad to get there. Certain occupants in the van had a little dig at the police escort now and again. Surprised we got there in one piece. A bobby followed us and drove my car to the nick as well.

We were thrown into a cell. On the sliding hatch, by the little door through which the police pass you food etc I found a bit of chalk, so drew a pig's face around the hatch area. Somebody would shout, 'OFFICER, QUICK!' and a bobby would stick his head through the hatch-hole and everyone would make grunting noises, like a pig. I felt a bit guilty about that later. The police were brilliant (Scunthorpe police). They offered us stew and chips, thought it was a joke at first, then a policeman came into the cell with a trolly, loaded with plates of stew and chips and even asked if we wanted second helpings!

In Scunthorpe police station it resembled the Black Hole of Calcutta. All the cells were overflowing with arrested miners. In our cell you either stood up or sat on the floor. Next door, we could here miners singing, *Arthur Scargill, Arthur Scargill, we'll support you evermore*, to the tune of a Welsh song. A policeman entered their cell and called a name out, for a miner to appear in front of a magistrate, but nobody answered. The officer called the name yet again and this time a voice replied 'I'm Spartacus!' whereupon another miner interjected by saying, 'No, I'm Spartacus!' and so on. It all felt so funny in the circumstances.

Later, we were led to the magistrates court by three, smartly dressed, policemen (CID) and our kid couldn't help having a dig: 'Where are you going tonight? Nightclubbing? Can you take us with you?' Well, one policeman took me on one side and asked me if it was my brother and I said it was. He told me to ask him to behave or the lads would take him into a cell and kick fuck out of him. I told Robert what he said. Stood in front of the magistrate and was bailed to appear again at a later date, so was released. Now, if this had been Nottinghamshire it would have been life sentences all round.

Wednesday, 25 July
Destination Babbington but couldn't get through. Chased by a transit van full of police at Pleasley but managed to escape. Found an old disused railway track, banking looked a bit steep so the lads got out of the car and I gave it a run, shooting up the embankment and then drove the car steady down the trackway which came to an end after a few hundred yards, a steep drop at the far end. The lads got back into the car and had the ride of their lives going down the steep slope but we escaped the police. Back to the Baggin, some food and home.

Thursday, 26 July
Destination Cresswell but didn't get through – coppers on the Clowne road had sealed it off again. Two thousand pickets did not get through.

Walking towards Bentinck: Shaun waves across the road to Darren (wearing cap) and Bob Wilson, 27 July 1984.

Friday, 27 July

Destination Bentinck Colliery, Notts.

Set off at 9 am. Went Chesterfield way and got as far as Kirkby in Ashfield but couldn't get any further. Walked two miles on the main road and over fields etc but we were surrounded by police and had to walk back. Made our way to the car and tried again. Stopped again. Set off walking again, getting to Bentinck Colliery about 11. 35 am. All the pickets were heading home so we started walking back. Darren shouted something at a copper who called him over, saying, 'Come over here, lad, I want a word with you'. Somebody shouted, 'DON'T GO!' which was good advice as Daz did not do as he was told. PC Plod then started shouting at him, saying he was 'A FOUL MOUTHED GIT.' Darren took his bright yellow shirt off, and Bob lent him his shirt. I got a lift back to the car from another picket and drove through the back roads to pick the lads up. Daz was a marked man but we all got back safely, to Silverwood Miners' Welfare.

Sunday, 29 July

Gay's mum had come up to see her on Saturday. I went to the docks, picketing at the Humber Bridge today, looking out for the movement of coal. Just me and Captain Bob Taylor. Gay has returned with her mother to London for a few days. Our poor little Suzanne, aged ten months, is just recovering from a broken collar bone. She was wearing a sling last week and yesterday after falling out of her baby-walker.

Monday, 30 July

Destination Cresswell? On days. Meeting at Baggin, 4 am. £6 petrol money.

Set off for the pit, big convoys of miners all over. Couldn't get through at first, all roads blocked at Clowne, Staveley etc but managed to get through to Bolsover Colliery. Went through Whitwell, picketed Bolsover, then walked a mile or so to Markham where there was a mass picket, must have been two thousand there. One pillock next to me and Shaun threw a brick through a bus window, top, front, offside. It left a clean, round hole. He hit the wrong bus anyway. Very quiet, no 'Zulu', just like earlier on at Bolsover.

Tuesday, 31 July

Newstead, South Notts. £9 petrol money. Managed to sneak through at Pleasley, 2–300 of us got through, the rest turned away but it was very very quiet.

V
Fighting the Drift Back to Work

August 1984

'... started picketing my own pit.'

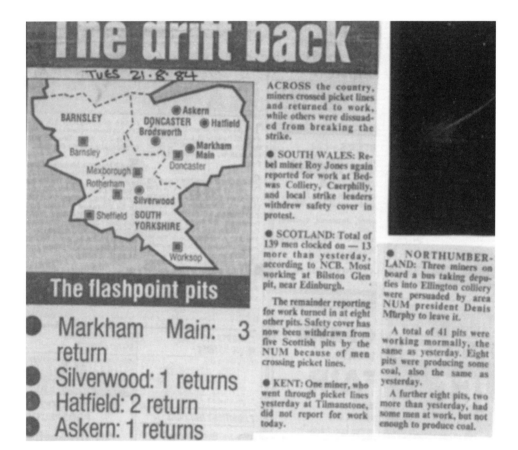

The drift back

TUES 21·8·84

BARNSLEY

Askern
DONCASTER   Hatfield
Brodsworth

Barnsley

Markham
Main

Mexborough
Doncaster

Rotherham

Silverwood

Sheffield   SOUTH
YORKSHIRE

Worksop

The flashpoint pits

● **Markham Main: 3 return**

● **Silverwood: 1 returns**

● **Hatfield: 2 return**

● **Askern: 1 returns**

ACROSS the country, miners crossed picket lines and returned to work, while others were dissuaded from breaking the strike.

● SOUTH WALES: Rebel miner Roy Jones again reported for work at Bedwas Colliery, Caerphilly, and local strike leaders withdrew safety cover in protest.

● SCOTLAND: Total of 139 men clocked on — 13 more than yesterday, according to NCB. Most working at Bilston Glen pit, near Edinburgh.

The remainder reporting for work turned in at eight other pits. Safety cover has now been withdrawn from five Scottish pits by the NUM because of men crossing picket lines.

● KENT: One miner, who went through picket lines yesterday at Tilmanstone, did not report for work today.

● NORTHUMBERLAND: Three miners on board a bus taking deputies into Ellington colliery were persuaded by area NUM president Denis Murphy to leave it.

A total of 41 pits were working mormally, the same as yesterday. Eight pits were producing some coal, also the same as yesterday.

A further eight pits, two more than yesterday, had some men at work, but not enough to produce coal.

The 'drift back to work' as summarised in a local newspaper, 21 August 1984. The official (NCB) figures apparently indicating a sole Silverwood miner and six others from the South Yorkshire/Barnsley and Doncaster areas. Sheffield Star

EDITOR'S SUMMARY

There was no let up for Bruce and his crew during the 'holiday' month of August, in fact it proved to be a very significant period for the miners of Yorkshire as well as in those on strike in other coalfield areas. Legal moves had begun on the first day of the month to seize the assets of the South Wales miners' NUM when they refused to meet a fine deadline. On 6 August two miners, Ken Foulstone and Robert Taylor, applied to the High Court for an area ballot. Whilst Bruce was struggling to repair his car on the 7th, there were major raids by pickets in Nottinghamshire, at Harworth and Silverhill; and also at the NCB's Doncaster offices, Coal House. The battlebus was soon on the road again, in Nottinghamshire, at Blidworth, and at Markham and Cresswell in North Derbyshire. Access to Scunthorpe was difficult due to police setting up strategic roadblocks and controlling bridges. The 'drift back to work' and all the associated NCB and biased media coverage caused understandable consternation and anger to Bruce and his mates who were more determined than ever to support their union. Towards the end of the month police and pickets clashed for five days at Easington colliery, Durham when a solitary picket went in to work. Bruce and his crew also found themselves picketing their own pit, in similar circumstances, getting up before dawn and receiving little sleep and no sympathy – just 'a battering' – from the police 'scab protection force'.

THE DIARY

Wednesday, 1 August

Welsh miners barricaded their union HQ in Pontypridd. Government anti-union laws fined them £50,000 for illegal secondary picketing of Llanwern Steel Works and Port Talbot.

Had a day off today. Heard that yesterday Pye Hill Colliery had gone on strike. The men want redundancy, but the management want to transfer them to other Notts pits which would meaning journeys to work of one and a half hours on a bus.

Thursday, 2 August

Cresswell, Derbyshire, our destination today. Got through at Worksop on the A60, ran a roadblock. A transit in front of us sped through, a copper went to kick the van, and missed, landing on his arse. We got through on the same basis but they did not follow us. Stopped in the village. A police officer threatened me and Shaun with arrest if we went into a shop for some cigs! Whatever next. We kept quiet today, one of those days when you think it is best to stay low key.

Friday, 3 August

Scunthorpe steelworks. £10 petrol money. Set off at 6 am. Coppers did not waste any time putting road

'SUPPORT YOUR UNION' poster issued by the NUM Yorkshire Area, asking members to unite in the wake of NCB's 'bribes'. NUM

NATIONAL UNION OF MINEWORKERS
(Yorkshire Area)

SUPPORT YOUR UNION

We congratulate all of you who have stuck out for so long against all odds. We recognise the hardship this has brought on you and your families, just as it has for miners and their families throughout the British Coalfield.

This struggle has cost us all too much hardship to turn back now. We appeal to every Yorkshire miner — stand together and we will win. In the Yorkshire Area, only a small handful of our men have returned to work. To those who have returned to work, we ask you to rejoin us.

No pit is safe — not any pit in the Yorkshire Area, no matter what coal reserves it has. Cortonwood has five years of good coal . . .

The Union's only strength comes from standing together. The Board has tried to bribe you with what is <u>already your money</u>.

Go back with the Union when we have won this great fight for jobs and a future! Then you will go back with pride, with your head held high and with the strength of your Union to defend your interests in the future.

TOGETHER WE WILL WIN! DIVIDED WE HAVE NO CHANCE !

JACK TAYLOR, President
OWEN BRISCOE, General Secretary
KEN HOMER, Financial Secretary
SAM THOMPSON, Vice-President
and the NUM Yorkshire Area Executive Committee

blocks up. Couldn't get through. Only three ways to get there and every one includes a bridge so it was a waste of time.

Monday, 6 August

£9 petrol money. Newstead, South Notts.

Stopped at Clowne strike centre and had breakfast – tea, eggs, bacon, tomatoes and a slice of bread for 25p. Got through without trying, through Pleasley but came across a jam sandwich (patrol car) so lads got down in the back of the car. Very quiet, picketing quiet these days and a bit boring. All lot of the good lads have been locked up – there are about 4,000 arrests.

Tuesday, 7 August

Bevercotes, £6 petrol money. Try and catch 'Silver Birch' (a young bloke who was a scab). Couldn't go, we had to wait and see a solicitor at 10 am. Car exhaust knackered, sat in Baggin etc etc. Went to Swinton Civic Hall for our dinner, cost just 10p.

Wednesday, 8 August

Hope things start brightening up on the picket line soon. Two scabs from Manton Colliery are taking the NUM to court, taking an injunction out to stop picketing. SCABBING BASTARDS! On telly they keep saying that they are Yorkshire miners but how can they be when they are from Worksop!

Leave Baggin at 8 pm. Can't go picketing. Gay and kids came back from mother-in-law's at 7.30 pm and I have to see a solicitor.

Been working on my car all day, exhaust been blowing, got a new middle bit but it is too short. On Tuesday night 300 pickets converged on Harworth Colliery when there were only 20 police on duty, some of them hospitalised. Pickets nearly flattened pit top, about 20 scabs' cars were damaged. Havoc caused, police got hold of maps from pickets showing pit locations etc. The police inspector thinks that it is the NUM who is organising all this trouble (all pickets carry a map), even me, wouldn't get far without one.

This morning a thousand pickets gathered at Harworth but the police were waiting for them. Some police vehicles were damaged and the cavalry was sent in etc etc.

PS. After Harworth, on Tuesday night, South Yorkshire pickets went to Silverhill, South Notts and went on the rampage. Forty scab cars were damaged. When they came out of work they were really sick; then it was Coal House, Doncaster when a few windows were broken. We missed out on a very busy day!

Thursday, 9 August

8.30 am, Baggin. Can't make it, due to meeting with solicitor. Anyway, my car exhaust has had it, my men sick as pigs, especially Shaun. The dark nights are drawing in soon, lighting up at 9.15 pm. Two weeks ago it was 10 pm. Soon will be winter.

Saw solicitor at Silverwood Miners' Welfare. Myself, our kid (Bob), Shaun and Bob Taylor stayed in. Solicitor just took a couple of statements. He was a union man, branch secretary for Maltby, and used to be a magistrate. His idea was to save the NUM money by not using solicitors too much as they were charging £30 an hour – so all of those that know something in the NUM are putting their brains into good use, doing statements etc. Today's destination was Bevercotes. The lads that did get through had to watch themselves as the police (from Essex) were in a mean mood.

To get things up to date:

Ken Foulstone and a chap called Bob Taylor (two working miners from Manton Colliery, Notts) went to London to take the NUM to court, for a ballot to take place, and withdraw pickets from Manton Colliery etc. Scabbing so and so's. What they really means is that they want to go to work but are frightened off crossing picket lines and want more scabs to join them. And they say it is a case of bringing democracy back into the Union. How many ballots do we need to have? What they mean is keeping having ballots until the result suits them. The minority should join the majority, and if not then get the NCB to bus them in. Notts have had their ballot and it went against a strike by a few thousand but they all went back to work – so if we had a ballot and voted by a majority for strike action they'd still go to work. The Government and MacGregor are going all out to break the strike but so far so good.

On the telly today they all keep saying that two Yorkshire miners are going back to work but they live and work in Notts; also there's a massive drift back to work in Staffs etc, about 200 more men have returned to work after their holidays. The NCB are drawing up plans to develop a £70 million mine in South Wales that might create 700 new jobs. The NUM are looking at this announcement sceptically and they do right to. It comes at a funny time. The plans for Marden have been on the books for years, so why announce it now? It's all a bit fishy. I bet Thatcher and her cronies are sweating now as the strike is solid in Yorkshire – involving 55 pits, including the Selby Complex. Mind you, as soon as Selby comes on stream a couple of dozen 'uneconomic' pits will go.

Northumberland: Solid
Scotland: Solid
Durham: Solid

Also, on telly tonight was a comment that 'the state of the mines are deteriorating' or could this be yet another propaganda exercise? After being on strike for nearly six months, some damage is not unexpected. The Government think that they are screwing us into the ground but it's the other way round. They are wanting to screw the entire working class, trying to rub us into the ground. They'll just have to keep trying.

Friday, 10 August
Blidworth Colliery, South Notts. £9 petrol money, Silverwood Welfare for 9 am.

Had a right game trying to get through, at least at first. A619 Worksop to Chesterfield sealed off; so we had to 'run a roadblock' and got through. Got to Pleasley, no coppers there, maybe somebody knows something! When we reached Blidworth we made our way onto the picket line but in front of us stood a giant policeman. He looked a bit like Bernard Breslaw, the *Carry On* actor. We shouted out, 'CAN THA EAT THREE SHREDDED WHEAT?' He looked very mean at first we got a smile from him. Quiet day. About 200 got through. Didn't get home until 2 pm.

'Silver Birch' [Chris Butcher] from Manton, a pit's top blacksmith? He's only worked there for five years and during the overtime ban worked seven days a week. Scabby Bastard! I think that says it all.

Monday, 13 August
Markham Main, near Chesterfield. £6 petrol money.

At 2 am forty cars set off from Silverwood Miners' Welfare but only twelve got through. We made our way to Swallownest, then on to Staveley Road. Absolutely no chance of getting through. Somebody knew something! After a lot of dodging, ducking and diving, we managed to get through – via the A19 at Worksop (Chesterfield Road). We found a side road. The police were using minimum deployment to block both ends of the road. There were lines of vans all over (police reinforcements). Finally arrived at Markham for 5 am. Not bad! We had negotiated fifteen miles of farm tracks over three hours. We decided to have a rest and a little sleep. Bob Taylor woke us up at 8.30 am – God, did we look rough, a car full of sleepy-eyed pickets. We had not been to bed that night, so felt wiped out.

It's a good job that we did not leave the car unattended. A hundred yards down the road several lads returning from picket duty found their car side windows smashed, and also the wiring under their dashboards ripped out. I wonder who could have done that?

Tuesday, 14 August
Destination today – Flixboro Wharf, Scunthorpe.

Set off at 7.30 am but no chance of getting through. Same again – three bridges controlled by thousands of police surrounding Scunthorpe. On the way back, at a roadblock on A18 I was driving steady & when I slowed Bob Wilson wound the window down and shouted out, 'WHAT'S THE MATTER NOW?' A thin copper put his hand in the car and slapped Bob in the face. Bob nearly jumped out of the car to get him! The policeman threatened to arrest me, confiscate my car and make us walk home. After that incident we got home OK. It's a good job the car door was between Bob and that copper. Bob has now developed a hatred of police in uniform. He can't abide them.

There's a lot of propaganda about miners returning to work. The NCB insist that a serious return to work is taking place. Last week, at Bilston Glen, 70 men were working. This week, according to the NCB, it is supposed to be 80. A third of them, safety men and then there is the office cat and her litter of six kittens. Gascoigne Wood, part of the Selby Complex – I've heard that a Yorkshire miner returned to work there, a loco driver. They'll be producing coal there next week – according to the NCB.

Wednesday, 15 August
Cresswell, Derbyshire, £5 petrol money.

Left Baggin at 9.30 am. There were 40 cars that left but only 5 got through. Notts/Derbys border practically impossible to pass, it was sealed off. But we got through, though we may have been the decoy. There were about 50 pickets already there. At Worksop, after getting through at the cement works, then the old pit yard (Steetley Colliery) we went down the A60 and encountered a roadblock. Bob Wilson shouted at the copper who pulled out his truncheon and started waving it about, then started laughing. He turned us back through Worksop. Finished up going back through the cement works, getting through at 11 am. Lads had to do the usual, get down in the back of the car as we passed by the coppers, parked up and watching us. They guessed we were pickets, well they could see me, but nobody was willing to stand in the middle of the road and stop me when I was doing 50 mph.

Thursday, 16 August
Cresswell, North Derbyshire, again. Set off from Baggin at 9 am. £5 petrol money. I pick up Captain Bob every night and we both go to the Baggin. From about 6 to 7 pm Eric Cassidy, our NUM treasurer, sits there. I went up to him and he showed me a piece of paper with our picketing 'target' written down, along with the departure time from the Baggin. There's no

talking – just in case the police employ some secret lip readers. Seriously, nobody trusts anyone and if a stranger comes into the club an NUM official will ask them to leave or maybe they would not be allowed entry in the first place. You just don't know who is who. I then sign for the petrol money and the picket money. I collect the lads' money and give it to them when I pick them up. Daz prefers to save his up until the end of the week, which, for him, is Friday. He doesn't buy any cigs – smokes everyone else's!

Picked the lads up as usual, Shaun last again, all bleary-eyed. Managed to get through OK. The police do not make it too hard for us when they realise that we are only going to Cresswell. It would be different if it was Notts! Had a look around. There were about 2–3,000 pickets. Gave it some scab but the scabs here are thick-skinned – they must be living on a different planet to us. Made our way back to the Baggin and had something to eat, then dropped the lads off and made my way home.

Friday, 17 August

Cresswell yet again. £5 petrol money and £1 picket money. Daz will be getting his £5 today – bet he is going out. When Bob Taylor and myself go to the Baggin for our orders every night there is only us two sat *without* a pint. We just have a cig. We're used to it now. Set off to Cresswell, car full. Finding it easier to get through but I still take 'short-cuts' such as disused rail tracks and farm lanes – just to make sure. When we got to the pit there was the usual police presence. Cresswell's a glum place – old, terraces of back to back houses and a pit literally in your back garden.

A couple of scabs went in, well walked in with their arms swinging and their snap bags in their hands. Some scabs still throw their snap into the pickets and go home. From what I can see, they must be bussing some of them through the back door. I never see more than a dozen or so scabs go in but I can only be in one place at a time. There are two entrances, about 300 yards apart. Got chatting to some other pickets. I was told that, coming down the motorway, there was an articulated lorry parked on the hard shoulder. The wind blew the back trailer door open and inside could be seen computers, telephone gear and women secretaries who could be seen sitting on stools, working on the computers. I was also informed that Cresswell was setting men on but they will still have to cross the picket line.

I went out tonight. Had a drink in the *Alpine* with my dad. I asked him if I could use his telephone. I phoned the *Sheffield Star* newspaper and asked them if they were interested in the news that the NCB was setting men on at Cresswell Colliery. They must have taken notice. In the *Star* a few days later the NCB announced that they were recruiting a few apprentices – craft apprentices such as electricians, fitters etc and they would not be required to cross picket lines. What they mean is they got found out, crafty bastards.

Sunday, 19 August

Went to a meeting at the Baggin. It was closed doors – no one was allowed unless they worked at Silverwood. Even the bar staff were checked. An official stood up and Bob Taylor was asked to leave. My team stood up and we said that Bob had been picketing for Silverwood since the start of the strike, so if he was excluded then so should we. Bob made for the bar. All he wanted was a pint – well it was Sunday afternoon – and he came back to sit with us. Anyway, there was no opposition to Bob staying, but we had to go through democratic procedures. He was allowed to stay, unanimously. He really was a Silverwood lad now! At the meeting were told that two Silverwood men would be going in tomorrow. They could arrive sometime between 3 am and 11 am, exact time unknown. So, it is picket duty at Silverwood from now on.

Monday, 20 August

Didn't sleep very well. Awoke at 11 pm and left home at 1.30 am and did the usual rounds, picking up the lads, Shaun being the last call – he lives nearest the pit, at East Herringthorpe. Parked at the *Reresby*. Some of the lads had nodded off! Gave them a shake and then we had a steady walk up the railway line. We came out at the bridge on Hollings Lane, having to climb a steep banking. Made our way to the NUM hut. The brazier was already lit but we couldn't get around the fire as it was too crowded. There was a good turn out this morning – plenty of us, plenty of police as well. I don't think that they were pleased to see us this morning. You can sense the atmosphere given off by the police. The scabs are going to go in and there's not a lot that we can do about it.

Police preparing to leave Silverwood Colliery after clashes with pickets when a lone miner reported for work on Monday. The miner who has not been named was, say the NCB, one of several in the Yorkshire Coalfield as a whole. In clashes between police and pickets later in the week, a number of arrests were made with both sides suffering injuries.

The so-called 'Silverwood Siege' followed picketing at the colliery when a lone miner returned to work on Monday, 20 August.
Rotherham Advertiser

17 Yorkshire miners defy pickets
PITS FURY AS MORE RETURN

TROUBLE erupted in the Yorkshire coalfield today as 17 strikedefying miners were confronted by thousands of pit gate pickets.

Today's return to work, though still only a trickle, was seen as a significant breakthrough by the Coal Board with seven new men crossing picket lines to work.

But pitmen's president Arthur Scargill immediately stressed that the majority of the region's miners were still supporting the strike.

The focus shifted from Silverwood and Gascoigne Wood pits to the Doncaster area where all pits had remained solidly behind the strike during the 24 weeks of the dispute.

Six men were reported back at work today at Markham Main, Askern and Hatfield Main collieries. And a seventh man turned back when 2,000 pickets blocked a Coal Board bus getting into Brodsworth colliery.

Barricades were set on fire at Hatfield pit as pickets failed to prevent two men starting work. A hundred police managed to hold back pickets and several men were arrested and one policeman slightly injured.

This headline from the Sheffield Star *of 21 August 1984 refers to '17 strikedefying* [Yorkshire] *miners' being 'confronted by thousands of pit-gate pickets'.* Sheffield Star

Tuesday, 21 August

After a meeting on Sunday started picketing my own pit. Got to Silverwood early. Don't know the time that the scab is going in. We were ambushed by riot police. They jumped out of their vans and set about about thirty of us. We got some right hammer.

Wednesday, 22 August

Silverwood. Got there for 3 am. Quiet. Police weren't standing for any nonsense this morning. Even if you talked too loud you might get some boot.

Thursday, 23 August

Overlaid! Apparently three men sneaked back to work at Kiveton Park Colliery yesterday.

Friday, 24 August

Destination Silverwood, for 3 am. £1 petrol money but had to push car home!

Monday, 27 August

Silverwood for 3 am. £1 petrol money. Quiet. Some lads put a tarpaulin up, and made a brazier to keep warm. It was a bit nippy this morning.

Tuesday, 28 August

Have been going to Silverwood for 3 am and going to the Baggin for orders between 6 and 7 pm, the previous evening. I'm not getting a lot of sleep. Sometimes I try and sleep on the settee, setting the alarm clock for 1 am. Can't help occasionally overlaying. Had some long days out from 1.30 am and not getting home until 2 in the afternoon. I'm tired but still look on the bright side. The boys in blue still expect us – they also have to be up all hours, peering over hedges, sitting in their cars and vans for hours, standing at roadblocks all over Nottinghamshire – just waiting for us! They don't know that we are not coming! That fresh air will do them good, keep them fit for the time when we bump into them again.

Wednesday, 29 August

Silverwood, 3 am. £1 petrol money. Quiet. Stayed until about 8 am, then went to Baggin and had a game of snooker, waiting for food parcels.

Thursday/Friday 30–31 August

Having a long weekend off.

This NCB leaflet extolling all striking miners to 'COME BACK TO WORK' even has a tear-off section to be returned to the colliery manager. Note the references to Christmas pay, debt and the 'necessary arrangements' that would be made. NCB

YOU AND WHO ELSE?

Men have started to go back to work at pits in every Area of the Yorkshire Coalfield – including South Yorkshire.

We know that more would like to join them but, understandably, don't want to face the "aggro" and the intimidation of being in a minority.

At almost every pit in the Area our managers are hearing the same thing, "We're not coming back in one's and two's. It would be different if there were a crowd of us".

Well here's the chance to come back on those terms.

This leaflet includes a Back to Work form and a reply paid envelope. If you genuinely feel that it's time to get back to work and would be willing to come back in a group all you have to do is fill in the form and post it in the envelope provided.

At any pit where there are enough men to form a sizeable group we will get in touch with you and lay on all the necessary arrangements.

ALL REPLIES WILL BE TREATED IN STRICT CONFIDENCE AND NO APPROACHES WILL BE MADE UNTIL WE HAVE ENOUGH NAMES TO MAKE UP A GROUP.

If you start work in the next couple of weeks your pay between now and Christmas (with holiday pay and other entitlements) will add up to more than £1000 for face men and about £800 for surface workers.

- If **YOU** think the strike has gone on long enough
- If **YOU** are fed up with waiting for a national settlement
- If **YOU** are facing mounting debts and dreading the final demands
- If **YOU** want to protect your job, your pit and your family's future,

THEN STAND UP FOR YOUR RIGHT TO WORK

Join the 50,000 British Miners who vote with their feet at the pit gates every day and

COME BACK TO WORK

- -

To: The Manager .... (insert name of Colliery or Unit)

I am interested in returning to work as part of an organized group.

Name: .... Check No. ....

Address: ....

.... Tel No (if any) ....

Signature: .... Date ....

VI
Battling at Silverwood
September 1984

*'... shouting, lights flashing
and police dogs barking.'*

SILVERWOOD N.U.M. BRANCH.

DEAR COLLEAGUES,

In line with the National Executive decision
of 30/8/84 we will be peacefully picketing our colliery
on Monday 3rd. September. We urge all our members to attend
this mass demonstration to show solidarity with the union
and contempt for the two scabs who have returned to work.

Demonstration will start at 3.30am. and again at 9.30am.

Yours fraternally,

President. *G Richa...*

Secretary. *D Matt.*

Delegate. *...*

Treasurer. *E C...*

*Silverwood NUM Branch letter, issued to members regarding 'peacefully picketing'/'mass
demonstration' at the colliery, to commence on Monday 3 September 1984.*

EDITOR'S SUMMARY

September in the coalfields was characterised by daily battles to try and keep the scabs out, especially in Yorkshire and Kent pits. On the 9th the NCB Chairman, Ian MacGregor, arrived at 'secret talks' with the NUM in Edinburgh wearing a Harrod's plastic bag over his head, a joke which he admitted in his autobiography that 'fell flatter than almost any antic I have pulled in my life.' The discussions broke down six days later and on the 22nd the Bishop of Durham referred to MacGregor as 'an imported elderly American'. Towards the end of the month NACODS voted by a majority of 82% in favour of strike and the High Court ruled the strike in Derbyshire as 'unlawful', and the Yorkshire strike as 'unofficial'. Bruce and his team continued their early morning picketing at Silverwood, often with excursions later in the day to nearby collieries such as Kiveton and Yorkshire Main where Bob Wilson was involved in an incident with a police motorcyclist. Maltby resembled a battleground on the 24th, with one man found badly injured and the local MP, Kevin Barron, experiencing at first hand how dangerous police versus picket confrontations could be. On the 27th, 'Bent Nails' succeeded in interrupting the convoy of police and scabs as did an opportunistic 'ambush' the next day. Remarkably, *The Sun* newspaper was not published on the 29th, the printers' union refusing to work since the editor had not overruled a journalist's reference to the Silverwood miners as 'scum'. Returning to the national scene, on the eve of the Labour Party Conference, on 30 September, Leader Neil Kinnock, was unable to stop motions of criticism concerning police actions during the strike. Peace was a long way off.

THE DIARY
Wednesday, 5 September
Silverwood, for 3 am. £1 petrol money. Picked the lads up and got to the pit on time. Quiet. Two men still going in. Returned home at 8 am.

A peaceful scene outside Silverwood colliery, September 1984. The NUM office (small detached brick building) can be seen on the left of the photograph, opposite the pit entrance. Bob Taylor

Thursday, 6 September

Same again, quiet, 'too quiet' but no trouble. We are not used to this. Mind you, it's a break for us. I'm getting fed up with my cigs – bought ten fags out of my picket money this morning and stood around the brazier to keep warm. I lit a cig and smoked it all myself – just fed up lighting up and passing the cig around and receiving a soaked tab back. They are good lads but I had to do it.

Friday, 7 September

Silverwood, 3 am. £1 picket money and £1 for petrol. Did a bit at Silverwood and then went to Kiveton Park, so got an extra £1 petrol money. When we arrived there we must have worn out the equivalent of two pairs of shoe leather. Got chased by the boys in blue. They just would not let us near the picket line this morning.

Monday, 10 September

Destination: Silverwood, 3 am, then to Kiveton. £1 petrol money. £1 picket money. Set off early again. Picked the lads up and parked at the *Reresby* as usual. Walked along the railway line. At the pit it was quiet, everyone smoking and supping tea. The tea hut opens early now, sells cigs for 10p each and you can get a cup of soup or a chip butty. I save my £1 picket money.

Gave it some scab when the scabs went in. There was a heavy police presence. The scabs arrive in a heavily armoured transit which doesn't half come flying down the pit hill – with a police escort.

Granville, our union man, gave me some extra petrol money (£1) and each of us lads another £1 picket money – a double shift again. If we did five double shifts it would be £10 each. I've been managing to save some money until the end of the week.

After Silverwood, made our way to Kiveton Park, passing through Swallownest etc. When we came to the main road, we turned right and parked among some houses, then started walking down the pit lane. As we got within a hundred yards of the pit entrance it was obvious that something had happened since dozens of pickets came running towards us, chased by a gang of police. We joined the pickets and ran with them as we could not just stand there and say to the police that we were doing nothing. We would have been fair game and perhaps arrested, charged with something or other. We wanted to avoid that and had been lucky so far. We dispersed and ran anywhere. I finished up running into a housing estate. The police began to thin out as they had chased us to their limits and we were well away from the pit entrance. I went down an alleyway and peered out. Just in front of me I could see a picket at the top of a banking, about fifteen foot high. He was hanging on to a tree and four bobbies were trying to grab his feet but every time they climbed up the banking they slipped back down. When they did reach him the picket kicked out for all he was worth, in fact one of his trainers came flying off. It was held by one of the bobbies who threw it away. They didn't get him as he managed to pull himself up and get away. The little incident made me smile. I met up with Shaun on the way back to the car and we then waited for the rest of the team. Everyone arrived back safely.

Tuesday, 11 September

Silverwood, 3 am; Kiveton Park, 5 am. £1 picket money and £2 for petrol.

Picked the lads up and stopped for a cup of tea at Bob Taylor's house. When I arrived a little late at Darren's, at Hollybush, Parkgate, he thought I had done a runner with the picket money! Stayed at Silverwood until 8 am and then moved on to Kiveton. There were about

3,000 pickets and no sign of the riot squad! What a change! Things looked like they were getting back to normal as we were on the front line, pushing and shoving – and giving it some 'Zulu'. Someone squirted something in a policeman's eyes. The pickets broke through in a surge but our path was blocked by the horses. It's a good job that there weren't too many police as Bob Wilson would have got some fist. He offered an Inspector and two policemen a fight. The Inspector told him to cool it, and then informed him that he was a 'marked man'. Bob reversed his clothes on his way back to the car, to avoid being recognised.

Wednesday, 12 September

MacGregor and Scargill in talks from last Sunday night. Monday, Tuesday and tonight as well. Both came out of the hotel. Arthur spoke, saying, 'It's a nice evening.' MacGregor turned round and replied, 'Yes, I agree.' Ha! Ha! Well, it's a start, anyway!

Silverwood for 3 am but was quiet although Johnny Dodds' son and two others were arrested in the wood. They were only looking for firewood, carrying a bow saw. From Silverwood we went to Swallownest Miners' Welfare for 5 am, destination Brookhouse Colliery. When we got there the coppers were on the bridge and the new relief road was sealed off. A gang of us set off walking on some old railway tracks and through a field, advancing to the pit over a lunar landscape of mounds and dips, lit by the moon. It was a full moon this morning, and on the picket line very quiet and still, too quiet for our liking. There were only 20–30 of us. As we got closer to the pit you could see something glinting, reflecting off the moonlight. There was no long grass, just an uneven series of spoil heaps, but high enough to hide behind. We continued to advance, thinking that surprise was on our side when, suddenly, about ten yards in front of us, a line of riot police stood up, their shields reflecting in the moonlight. We could see the dark outline of their uniforms and big perspex shields. Then they charged! There was no shouting and little noise. A copper on the bridge put his searchlight on us as we ran through the field. It was a unnerving experience. We managed to make our way back to the bridge. You could still see them, knelt down in the dark, shields catching occasional reflections from the moonlight and street lamps. They weren't taking any prisoners today! Felt very wary after this, so we had a quiet morning later.

Thursday, 13 September

Silverwood for 3 am. Waiting for the big one. Will it come? Had a push. Young Craig Dimbleby, Daz's mate, was arrested. Eric Cassidy, our NUM treasurer, had a word with the police and they released Craig.

Deputies are voting today, about the NCB instructing them to cross picket lines – in armoured buses if necessary. Kiveton and Kellingley deputies have gone on strike. A lot of Yorkshire deputies have had their wages stopped. At the beginning of the strike MacGregor told the deputies that he did not expect them to cross picket lines if they were subjected to intimidation or violence. The deputies at Silverwood reckon that the two scabs going in will be transferred to Harworth.

Picket duty now from 3 am to 8 am at Silverwood. Police are taking the scabs in at different times. Orders are now for us to put Silverwood first for picketing – but when the scabs go we can go to either Kiveton or Brookhouse and other nearby venues.

After Silverwood we went flying to Yorkshire Main (Edlington]. We turned left at the *Cecil* pub, approaching the pit from the Doncaster end. I haven't seen so many pickets since Harworth and Orgreave, must have been three or four thousand present. Had trouble in

A crowd of pickets and police in the Silverwood pit yard/entrance, Thursday 13 September 1984.

Working miners leaving Silverwood receive the wrath of local striking miners and residents. Note the police Transit escort. John Harris/IFL

trying to park the battlebus. The lads couldn't wait to get out. Swarms of pickets walking up the road so we joined them. We then marched forwards but in the distance, marching towards us were masses of pickets! The pit entrance was in the middle of both groups. Looked like no one would be going to work today. After half an hour a police convoy came up from behind us, a few dozen Transits, a couple of Range Rovers and some motorbike police, all moving slowly. We parted and let them through – looks like they overlaid this morning! Caught them on the hop. As they drove into the pit yard the driver of an articulated lorry was stuck in all the pickets (the road was thronged with pickets for hundreds of yards). The lorry driver wound his window down and shouted to us, asking to be let through. Everybody parted and moved on to the causeway. He managed to drive through OK. As the lorry moved off our kid [Bob Wilson] looked round and coming up behind him was a policeman on a motorbike. As he slowly drove past our kid gave his back wheel a kick. The police motorcyclist carried on, but he was veering all over the place and nearly came off. It's a good job that there were thousands of us, or I'm sure that Bob would have been nicked [but see later entry, 14 December 1984].

Considering that there were thousands of pickets this morning it was very quiet. There weren't many police in the pit yard, maybe fifty of them but it was a good morning's picket and no real violence. The police kept a low profile.

Friday, 14 September
Got to Silverwood for 3 am. Scabs went in at 3. 40 am. On the way to pick up Bob Taylor I was stopped by the police. Our Bob heard them on the radio asking if a brown Triumph 2.5 was stolen. When I got to his house, Greenpiece Cottage, at Haugh (Manor Farm), near Rawmarsh, he had the kettle on.

It was quiet at Silverwood. Then we went to Cresswell, Derbyshire – and about time. The police had all the roads well and truly blocked but managed to get through, about 200 of us altogether. I think the Union hopes to catch the police off guard. Hope we get into Derbys/Notts more regular now. The police turned back 600 cars on the A1, heading for Bevercotes. They'd had re-elections after police would not let striking miners who worked there, through to vote last time.

Four lads were arrested at Silverwood last week. One was kept at Armley Jail, Leeds and came out a nervous wreck. The police got them to sign statements saying that they were going to ambush scabs, the police charging them with 'conspiracy to murder'. Bleeding stupid carry on. That's what we are up against … and that slimy Leon Brittan.

I heard today that the Chief Constable of Yorkshire has banned *shield banging* !

Saturday, 15 September
Talks between the NUM and NCB broke down after a few hours on Friday. Arthur Scargill is right: Thatcher has got her finger in the pie. She has got it to come one day. The Government has ordered millions of candles. Wonder if she will call the troops in to shift coal stocks in a month's time.

I wonder which pits the scabs will be going into the next time? I hope it is a Scottish pit. If it is, then Thatcher has picked a good adversary.

There is a big march through Barnsley today. Arthur Scargill and other union leaders and supporters there.

Looks as though it is going to be a long and hard winter.

A man walking his dog in Parkgate [near Rotherham] the other day was approached by four policemen who told him that they had seen *his dog* on the picket line at Silverwood last week! The man wasn't even a miner. They told him that if they saw the dog on its own it would be going to the fire station. The other week one picket at Silverwood kicked one of the scabs' cars as he was going in to work. The police arrested the picket but then released him, otherwise they would have got some right hammer – they were outnumbered, their mates being higher up the hill. The scab had informed the police of the picket's identity. When the lad came out of the East Dene Club on Saturday night the police were waiting for him. They locked him up, breathalised him and gave him some fist.

MacGregor said on telly tonight that he refuses to resume talks with the NUM until the violence on the picket lines stops. Ha Ha, the little fat b..........!

Princes Diana gave birth to a baby boy at 4.20 pm today.

Who is going to get screwed to the ground? The NUM or Thatcher? I wish people would open their eyes and see what is really going on – and I don't mean the pickets.

Monday, 17 September
Overlaid, and glad I did as I did not like the idea if being sent to Maltby.

Tuesday, 18 September
Silverwood, 3 am. Had a good run today. Quiet, not many pickets. Then to Kiveton Park for a mass picket. Six arrests. Gave it some 'Zulu!' Nearly broke through the police ranks but they sent the horses in. Two hundred miners picketed a scab miner's house a hundred yards from the pit. The police shouted, 'GO HOME!' Bob shouted to the police inspector, 'YOU ARE STOPPING HERE YOU BASTARDS BECAUSE WE'RE NOT GOING YET.' The inspector said to him, 'What did you say?' Bob, being at the front of the picket line and therefore in a vulnerable position, replied, 'You're stopping here, because we are going nowhere.' What else could he say when in a vulnerable, threatening situation like that?

From Kiveton we moved on to Yorkshire Main at Edlington. There were 2–300 pickets but no trouble. Five or six scabs went in, riding on a bus. Returned to Silverwood. Changed menu – had some soup and then some chips. Heard that eighteen police horses were being sold for dog meat.

ACAS meeting between the NUM and the NCB to hear both sides of the story.

Four men stopped going in to work at the Selby Complex. Might see some new picketing soon.

Thatcher had a meeting with her 'War Cabinet' the other day. A fight to the finish, she says. It'll be her finish, touch wood.

Wednesday, 19 September
Silverwood, 2 am. £3 petrol money.

Scabs are going in early now, 2.20 am. No trouble today. Went flying to Kiveton, a small picket there, then back to the Baggin for some snap.

Thursday, 20 September
Silverwood, for 3 am. Scabs went in early again. There were about 50 pickets. All quiet this morning. Stayed until about 8. 30 am, to see them going home. Gay's uncle Jim, a bobby from the Hertfordshire Constabulary, has been drafted into the picket lines of South Yorkshire. He did not want to come, and he's fed up and wants to go home. I think he is at Maltby, God bless him. Mass picket at Brookhouse this morning. We went there but missed the scabs as they

went in early. 'Ordinary' police were there at first, then the riot squad arrived, pushing us all up the lane. Not too much trouble though, just a few bricks thrown.

Friday, 21 September
Found out that the police were going to Silverwood and then Brookhouse: we are all following each other. Quiet at Silverwood, so went on to Kiveton.

Moved on to Maltby.

Getting rather fed up, all this running about, chased all over.

The police have a new toy: a Transit with 'wings' on – large guards on either side of the vehicle. They drive up the road slowly, under cover of their 'guarded transit', batons at the ready. Their job is to clear the roads and disperse the pickets.

Daz, Bob Wilson and myself went into the woods, passing timber, anything we could move, to other pickets who were constructing a barricade. It was a quiet day. Got back to the Baggin safe and sound and had some food.

Heard that over the weekend two CID men in a Chinese take-away were beaten up by lads in Maltby.

Sunday, 23 September
A big meeting in the Baggin at noon. Every Tom, Dick and Harry was there – some men I have not seen for six months! We were told we had to be careful.

Monday, 24 September
Silverwood this morning, for 1.30 am. Drove up to the pit. The bottleneck bridge on Hollings Lane, above the railway line, had twenty police on it. They would not let us through so we had to go back down the lane and park at the *Reresby* pub car park. Walked it to the pit, keeping away from the police on the bridge but the scabs had already gone in by the time we arrived. Walked back down the lane, to the car, and made our way to Maltby. It turned out that we did not get our mass picket today at Silverwood.

Parked in the *Lumley Arms* car park at Maltby with a full crew this morning and set off walking to the pit. It was still pitch black and not very well lit where we were. The closer that we got to the pit entrance the darker it was, no street lights or anything. We noticed a big boulder in the road which seemed silly as it could kill someone and is nowhere near the police lines. Suddenly, we heard a car approaching. I thought to myself, I hope he sees the great boulder. A small Fiesta appeared and swerved right at the last second, veering all over the road but then carried on. We moved on to the pit and made our way to the front line. I had in my possession some polished aluminium plate, about three inch square, with a mirror-type finish. I gave some of these to the lads and the rest was thrown at the police. In the gateway, every morning that we came here, an officer would shine great spotlights on us, really blinding lights, so you could not see. That's why I had the polished plates. When the spots hit

Bruce Wilson's letter puts a picket's point of view in regard to 'missile throwing', via a letter publishing in the Rotherham Advertiser, *21 September 1984.*

us I pointed my plate at the lamp. It worked! The policeman switched it off, then turned it on again. We showed our mirrors and he got the reflection back and then gave up, so it definitely worked. Those few hours in the shed, making them, paid off. It was quiet, still and dark on the front line. There were rows of police in front of us. We turned round and saw that there were many miners behind us. We were getting ready for a push when, several yards away, I heard 'Razzer', a Silverwood lad, shout out, 'BADGE COLLECTORS TO THE BACK', and there was laughter all over, and responses such as, 'WHAT THA FUCKING ON ABOUT, I'M HERE AREN'T I?' Things then got heated. A few bricks were launched, then a few more and that was it – the police charged! I jumped over a wall and then jumped straight back again. The riot squad were hiding, they did not get me but it was a close shave. Things went quiet so we decided to have a look around. With Shaun, and Daz I went for a walk into the wood to see if we could get round the police front line. Only got a few yards when Shaun shouted to me, 'LOOK AT

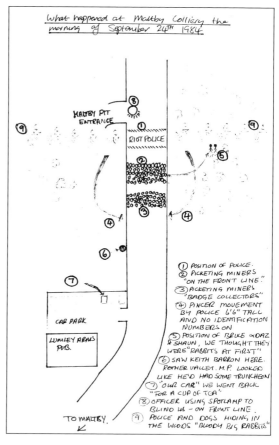

This sketch map was produced by Bruce Wilson in order to supplement his diary entry of 24 September 1984 when police clashed with pickets at Maltby.

THEM RABBITS!' We could see several pairs of eyes peering at us through the darkness but the eyes were about four foot from the ground. We saw the dog-handlers just in time. 'Bloody big rabbits!' I said to Shaun, retreating quickly from the wood.

Stood on the front line for a while and then, I don't know why, but I decided to go back to the car and have a cup of tea from my flask. We all went back to the *Lumley Arms* car park for a drink of tea. As we sat there all hell was let loose. Miners came running back up the road towards the village. We got out of the car to have a look, walking back towards the pit entrance. We could see them, within spitting distance, they had done a dirty trick – the snatch squads had performed a pincer movement and flanked the pickets, trapping about thirty lads on the road. The police came out of the woods. There was nowhere for them to go! There were police dogs and their handlers still in the woods behind them and at the side of them. The police went wild and truncheoned anything that moved. Big bastards they were, all a good 6 foot 4 inch tall, wearing yellow jackets with no identification markings – they must have been Coldstream Guards on manoeuvres!

We came across one lad who was unconscious – fractured skull (?) and blood all over him. A copper stood on him while three others laced into him. One man [Kevin Clegg?] went to help but one of the policemen threw him on one side and he was told to 'Fuck off'. [The badly injured man was probably Ian Wright, who was not a miner, a member of the Hammersmith Miners' Support Committee] The Coppers were charging about but were not wearing identification numbers. It was the same old story – pickets treated like animals.

When walking back to the car I came across the Rother Valley MP Kevin Barron, also making his exit. It looked like he had had some boot and truncheon for good measure. The police will grossly exaggerate what went on today. Their purpose will be to slag the pickets, so that they can arm themselves with rubber bullets. Can't call it heavy fighting today. It was Kevin Barron, badge collectors and pickets who got clobbered this morning!

Tuesday, 25 September

Destination Silverwood. Picked lads up and went up to the *Cavalier* for a change and then walked down to the pit. It was quiet on the front line. Ordered to go to Kiveton – well, instructions to go there were issued but there was nobody around, everyone had apparently gone to Barnburgh. When we arrived there at at 6 am the scabs had gone in. There were about 500 pickets. From what I saw, it looked like an ideal battleground, probably another Orgreave – plenty of open fields and woods. Wonder if the police think the same.

Deputies voted yesterday, and also today and tomorrow. According to sources at Silverwood the

Pit police accused of beatings

TWENTY-FOUR people were injured as police clashed with thousands of pickets in fresh scenes of violence at trouble-torn Maltby yesterday.

After the latest incidents, which came as a handful of men went into work at the colliery, accusations flew over police behaviour — likened by one onlooker to that of animals.

A member of Sheffield Police-watch said they had attacked people without provocation and gone looking for blood, not arrests.

But police replied that they were subjected to an almost continuous barrage of missiles, and said airguns had been used against them.

One picket was detained in Rotherham District General Hospital and nine other people were treated for injuries received in incidents around Maltby colliery.

They included Rother Valley MP, Kevin Barron, who said he was truncheoned four times by two policemen who attacked him as he walked to his car.

His left arm was in a sling and badly bruised, he said.

"It was a totally unprovoked assault. Twelve police armed with shields and truncheons came out of the woods and started lacing into everybody. There was no attempt to make arrests.

"I had just spent two hours trying to persuade people not to throw stones at the police. I admit I was not 100pc successful.

"When this happened, nothing was going on. One chap was eating a sandwich.

"The police were bludgeoning

Injured MP Kevin Barron

people to the ground. When I went back later there was still a pool of blood on the pavement. I have never seen anything so brutal in my life."

Police said a Range-Rover ambulance was attacked and damaged near the colliery and half-inch-square lead pellets were fired by catapult, landing 100 yards back from police lines. Fourteen officers were hurt, two were taken to hospital.

Police estimated there was a maximum of 5,000 pickets there. Seven men went into work. The NUM put the number of pickets at 1,200.

Policewatch member Paul Foun-

tain said he arrived at the scene about 4.30 a.m. Reports of continuous stoning were exaggerated. A couple of dozen stones were thrown, but this stopped when Mr Barron appealed, he said.

He alleged he was narrowly missed by a stone thrown back from the police ranks.

When the police advanced through woodland to surround the pickets, he saw sights he hoped he would never see again.

"They were just like animals. They went wild," he claimed.

One man he saw truncheoned to the ground then kicked. Truncheons were flying everywhere. The police were not going for arrests, he said.

A man was lying with a deep gash in his head and Mr Fountain thought he must have lost a pint of blood.

Chief Constable Peter Wright said he had received an official complaint from Mr Barron and that it would be investigated.

Mr Barron said the squad of police officers were wearing boiler-suits without identification numbers. This might make it difficult for him to identify the ones who assaulted him.

The Chief Constable admitted yesterday that the police unit wearing boilersuits did not have identification numbers, but said arrangements were in hand to have numbers put on them.

He added: "It was a very nasty situation at Maltby this morning. If Mr Barron says he was going to his car, I cannot dispute that with him. But the police manoeuvre was aimed to disperse stone throwers.

"The point has been made that the wrong people came into contact with police and that was not my view of it.

"If you are not party to that sort of behaviour then the best thing to do is to go away."

On the Policewatch allegations, he said: "This type of general allegation is easy to make and difficult to answer.

"At Maltby this morning there was severe disorder with the police subject to a constant bombardment of stone-throwing over a period of hours. Ten arrests were made."

The local newspaper report concerning the 'scenes of violence' at Maltby colliery includes contrasting opinions from the police and the Sheffield Policewatch organisation. The injured MP Kevin Barron is also featured. Rotherham Advertiser

115

majority are for strike action. If all the North votes a majority then all that is needed in the moderate coalfields is an even vote, then they will be out. We will have to wait and see. Energy Secretary Peter Walker says on telly, with a complacent smile on his face, that the deputies will be back at work in a few days. He will probably give them what they want – but, with the NUM, well that is a different matter.

Wednesday, 26 September
Does your feet reach the end of those boots lad?

Early start. Silverwood for 2 am. Quiet this morning, no hassle, no chasing about, just nice and steady on the picket line. Someone had given Barney a new pair of pit boots but they were miles too big. A Silverwood lad, Barney, is just 4 ft 10 inches in his stocking feet and speaks in a high-pitched voice. Everyone knows him. The police were facing us and one of them asked Barney if his feet touched the end of his boots. Quick as a flash, Barney replied, 'Does thy 'ead touch top of thy 'elmet?' That shut the bobby up. There were great howls of laughter.

Left after scabs went home. Parked the car as normal, outside our house. A police car was parked at the end of our road, only a few feet away. One of the occupants shouted to me, 'SHIFT THAT CAR!' I started walking away from my car and the bobby shouted, 'I'M NOT GOING TO TELL YOU AGAIN. MOVE IT!' I asked him why. He told me that I was 'double-parked' (there was a car across from mine, but not causing any difficulty for anyone wanting to pass by). He informed me that I would be nicked unless I moved my car down a bit, the

A bleary-eyed Bob Wilson comes to the door of his cottage, following an early call from brother Bob.

clever bastard. He then warned me that I would get ten years 'hard labour' as well, and he wasn't smiling when he said it. Never mind, tomorrow is another day.

Sat watching telly at home later. On *Look North* they were interviewing a man who had gone back to work at his pit. When asked why he had gone back, he said, 'My neighbours sent round a bag of bones for the dog but I cooked them for the family instead, and we ate them. That's why I went back to work.'

Thursday, 27 September

3 am, Silverwood. Set off early this morning. Daz and Shaun were off-duty this week. Called for Bob Taylor and picked up my brother, Bob, from his home, Greenpiece Cottages, Manor Farm. When I knocked at his door he wasn't too pleased, not so much due to me knocking him up, but because he had been burgled the day before. All they took was a food hamper that he had won in the pub's tote draw. It's a bit sad when some bastard nicks the only food you have got in the house. Anyway, we set off for Silverwood, in total darkness. Bob queried the route that I was taking since usually we travelled via Thrybergh and up Hollings Lane but today I drove by the *Cavalier* and down the road to the pit. I parked in the colliery car park and then we walked up to the nice fire there. We stood around an old oil drum with a fire in it, just across from the pit gates and next to the 'cig hut'. There was panic from the police and from the scabs. Someone had put 'foreign objects' on the road, causing punctures to several police vehicles. The police surrounded the scabs, thinking that they would be ambushed. It slowed them down this morning.

Captain Bob refuses to part with his Deed of the Day medal. Looks like I will have to make some new ones!

We stayed for another few minutes, said our good-byes to the other pickets.

The police will have to walk down from the pit entrance to the *Reresby* and then up to the *Cavalier* at Ravenfield, carrying torches to check the road surface. They will not be pleased with the situation and things will no doubt be hard for us all for some time, maybe even making us douse the picket fire with buckets of water.

Friday, 28 September

Ambush at Silverwood.

After collecting the lads (brother Bob, Captain Bob, Daz and Shaun) we left the Baggin at 1 am and parked at back of the *Reresby*. There were convoys of pickets' cars

Sketch map produced by Bruce Wilson in order to explain some of the events that took place outside and near to Silverwood Colliery on 28 September 1984.

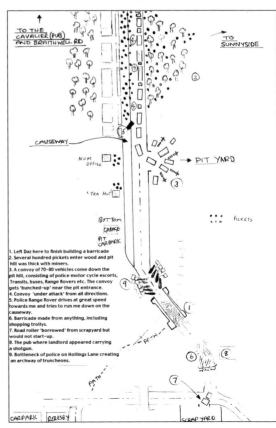

1. Left Daz here to finish building a barricade
2. Several hundred pickets enter wood and pit hill was thick with miners.
3. A convoy of 70–80 vehicles come down the pit hill, consisting of police motor cycle escorts, Transits, buses, Range Rovers etc. The convoy gets 'bunched-up' near the pit entrance.
4. Convoy 'under attack' from all directions.
5. Police Range Rover drives at great speed towards me and tries to run me down on the causeway.
6. Barricade made from anything, including shopping trollys.
7. Road roller 'borrowed' from scrapyard but would not start-up.
8. The pub where landlord appeared carrying a shotgun.
9. Bottleneck of police on Hollings Lane creating an archway of truncheons.

all over. We had to wait for ages at Aldwarke Lane for all of them to go by. It was a mass picket. From the car park we walked along the railway line and could hear a commotion on the bridge. When we got there, pickets were building a barricade so we stopped and helped them for a while; then me and our kid walked up to the pit and left Daz to finish building the barricade with the other pickets. Saw Robin Walker and Mick Tracy. Don't think they liked the action. We got to the NUM office and stood there for ten minutes. The uniformed police withdrew and were replaced by the riot police. As they left (changed over) they made one arrest, dragging a lad away – just for swearing. We then made our way up the pit hill. Some pickets started building a barricade, using material taken from walls and two pillars were placed in the road. I carried on walking up the hill for about a hundred yards. Several hundred pickets went into the woods near the Sunnyside area; but the pit hill was still full of miners who were also on the causeway and close to the road, spread all the way up the hill.

A convoy of 70–80 police vehicles started coming down the hill, like a never ending stream, including motorbikes and new Range Rovers, some of them with their sides already dented. There were also green buses full of Met police, their interior lights switched on. The convoy slowed and bunched up near to the pit entrance so it was an opportunity not to be missed – everyone (and there were hundreds of miners on the causeway and in the woods, on either side of the road) felt exactly the same. They were met with a barrage of missiles, a motorbike cop was kicked and nearly came off, van windscreens were smashed and coach windows were damaged. One coach had all its windows smashed down one side. One idiot put an ambulance window through. The noise of the glass shattering was unbelievable. The macho Met men could be seen, their heads between their knees, covered with shards of glass. A police Range Rover came at me at great speed and tried to run me down, coming on to the causeway in the process. I had jumped into some bushes just in time or might have been seriously hurt or killed. The police got what they deserved. Our 'ambush' was not planned, it was just an opportunity, a provoked opportunity, not to be missed. They were sitting ducks and we needed to take out our frustrations today. The London Met wore smart, double-breasted black uniforms with silver buttons and white shirts but they were not so smart today. The police are brave in numbers with all their riot gear and the law is always on their side and they can not do anything wrong even if it is wrong but we gave them some of their own medicine -and we are then supposed to be guilty and feel guilty. We'll have to be careful now.

After the riot police charged up the hill. Some of us escaped into the woods. When we got to the top of the hill we were outnumbered by the police who managed to split us into two groups;then they started pushing us about, clearing the road etc. We were forced all the way up to the *Cavalier* pub.

Many pickets just got into their cars and went back home or got completely out of the way. After clearing the roads the police pushed what was left of us down Braithwell Road. A police Range Rover came up behind us but he did not stay very long. I heard the screech of his brakes as he reversed and turned away, avoiding the stones that were aimed in his direction.

We made our way back to the pit. On a small, about two-foot high wall near the garage, at the top of the hill, an elderly miner was sat down. A riot cop told him to move. He refused, so got a smack on the side of his face. I did not see what the copper hit him with but the old man dropped to the ground like a stone. A copper wielding a truncheon then stood over him. Twenty or so pickets lost their rag at this point and chased this copper who ran for the security of his mates. Pickets then ripped up walls, gates etc and made another barricade across the road.

Decided to make my way to the pit gates but, with Bob Taylor, Bob Wilson and two other Silverwood lads, was kept in a field by the road. Crossed the road at the bottom of the hill and there were police all over, it was swarming with them. A bunch of about twelve riot police were in front of us.

We made our way into the fields at the bottom of Spencer Drive. We were a bit scared of going into the pit woods situated at both sides of the lane but we crept in and came upon a van full of riot police. We lay in the grass and waited, but not for long as the police van moved away, so we set off again. We kept meeting groups of men in the wood so we would shout, 'PICKET!'. Bumped into Granville Richardson and Jim Devine, NUM officials and got some petrol money. Everyone is flying to Maltby from here but we are going home to bed. Got back to the car, Daz was already there, with Captain Bob who had had to scale a tree to escape from the police! Bob heard that battling was taking place at the bottom of the pit lane, near the *Reresby* and there were shopping trolleys scattered all over the place. Paul Burke nicked a road-roller from the scrapyard, started it up but couldn't get it to stop! The landlord of the pub came out with a shotgun! Amazing scenes. Chief Supt. Nesbit was struck on his shoulder by a paint pellet and ran for safety. A police dog attacked one picket. Should have realised it was going to be a battle zone today as Kate Adie, the BBC War Correspondent was also here!

Later, we found out that the miners who walked over the bridge on Hollings Lane had to face an archway of police, wielding truncheons. They pushed the miners down the lane and made as many pickets as they could find walk under the 'arch', so the lads got a real battering, including Ian 'Mitch' Mitchell and Daz.

Heard that two scabs are going in at Manton Colliery [Worksop] on Monday. Haven't got the guts to admit they want to work. They keep calling for a ballot, two of them in particular: Bob Taylor (not our Bob!) and Ken Foulstone have even taken their own union to court. Looks as though there could be a lot of casualties at Manton on Monday.

YORKSHIRE NUM – NO SURRENDER!

Saturday, 29 September

The Sun newspaper was not published today as the printers' union refused to work since the journalists had used the word 'SCUM' to describe the miners. The editor had rejected a demand by production workers for 'SCUM' to be removed.

The first newspaper cutting refers to the unusual non-appearance of The Sun *newspaper on 29 September and the second consists of an eye-witness report from Sam Franklin of the Sheffield Policewatch group.*

1

● The Sun newspaper failed to appear today after the editor rejected a demand by production workers that the word "SCUM" be removed from a page one editorial on the ambush of police at Silverwood colliery, near Rotherham.
The workers then refused to publish the newspaper.

2

Sam Franklin, of the Policewatch group, said three observers saw the incidents at Silverwood yesterday.

He rejected the suggestion that the events had been planned: "From the picket side, it was entirely disorganised. No one knew what was going on at all, it was complete chaos. As far as I saw, there was no ambush.

"The only organised violence I saw was by the police."

He added: "Most of the police ignored calls for first-aid, and the ambulance took at least 20 minutes to arrive, by which time one injured picket had lost consciousness.

"Pickets were angry at the delay because they thought it had been deliberately held up by police."

VII

Cavalry Charges and Riot Squads at Brodsworth and Rossington

October 1984

*'… missiles went over that thick it was like
a flock of starlings flying overhead.'*

A typical Brennan cartoon of the period, taken from the October strike issue of the Yorkshire
Miner.

EDITOR'S SUMMARY

At the same time as all the disturbances and bitter exchanges between pickets, scabs and police further attempts were being made to undermine the National Union of Mineworkers through the courts. On 10 October the High Court imposed a £200,000 fine on the miners' union plus a £1,000 on its president for contempt of court and by the 25th the union's funds were ordered to be seized. Talks via ACAS began on 11 October but ended four days later, the great barrier continuing to be interpretation of 'uneconomic' pits. Much of the press may have been critical of Arthur Scargill but MacGregor himself was seen by many as a barrier to progress. Raymond Seitz, an American attaché in the US Embassy, quoted in John Campbell's new biography of Margaret Thatcher, *The Iron Lady*, wrote that MacGregor represented management with all the political and social sympathy of a bar-room bouncer.... I recall cringing whenever he was on television'. The 'Yankee butcher' image rang true. Support of the strike from NACODS waned from the 25th, following the NCB's revision of the colliery review procedure. Bruce and his friends continued to vent their anger on the few scabs going in to work at Silverwood and Kiveton Park collieries and were eager participants in a battle of wits and fitness at Brodsworth Main on 12 October. There was light relief the day after, via a session of potato picking, followed with a journey to North Derbyshire and considerable Silverwood continued to be the main location for Bruce and his mates. Even 'Captain Bob' being truncheoned for nothing more than minding his own business, did not deter or lessen the determination to follow union picketing instructions. By the end of an eventful October there were now 7,428 arrests and 49 imprisoned during the eight-month strike.

THE DIARY

Monday, 1 October

Back to the old ways: collected orders from Baggin at 7 pm, destination Silverwood. It was very quiet when we got there, although some Maltby lads reckon that the coppers are waiting for revenge after the incidents at Silverwood last Friday. Just before the scabs arrived the police started to emerge from the pit gates. One started feeling feint and four of his mates carried him back into the pit yard. Maybe he couldn't face the front line.

Decided to move on to Thurcroft pit. Got chased around the housing estate, wearing another pair of shoes out.

Tuesday, 2 October

Decided against Silverwood as I thought there might be some action at Thurcroft. Arrived at 5 am. Policeman with a microphone informed us that the scabs had already gone in. He was lying. The cavalry, riot squad and hundreds of uniformed police pushed us towards the bridge on the M18. I was forced to run down an embankment, chased by some coppers carrying shields and batons. Had to run across the motorway to escape. Someone told me later that I was seen on telly. I was wearing my maroon lumberjack jacket. The police took charge of the bridge but they got stoned, one of them getting a direct hit.

I've heard that a writ has been issued against Arthur Scargill, for him to appear in court on Thursday. So far he has ignored such 'requests'. Looks like he could be threatened with jail and the NUM funds sequested. Late on at Thurcroft, policeman in charge shouted, 'IF YOU WANT YOUR CARS BACK YOU'VE GOT FIVE MINUTES TO GET THEM!' Clever Bastard. I walked back through police lines, ever fearful of a trap. They nicked eight lads as we were making our way back to the cars, selected at random.

Picking coal from old tips and quarries, even new outcrops, was an essential activity for many miners as the winter progressed. Arthur Wakefield

Wednesday, 3 October

Orders for today: Kiveton Park, for 5 am. £3 petrol money.

Did not walk down to the bridge entrance as we would get penned in as usual. Stopped on the top road. Coppers tried to round us up but we sneaked around the back but finished up back at square one. It was quiet on the South Yorkshire front. I'm having trouble with my battlebus – crankshaft going, plus loads of other noises.

Thursday, 4 October

Kiveton Park, 11 am. £3 petrol.

Caught the coppers on the hop. A few hundred pickets had turned out. Scabs were taken out the Harthill way, via the bottom gate, near the bridge.

Went to Swinton Civic Hall for some dinner.

Deputies are still talking. I don't think that they will ever come out. Looks like it is going to be a long and hard strike. At home we have got enough coal for a few weeks.

After picket duty this week our kid (Bob), Daz and myself went digging for coke at British Steel, Aldwarke, near Rotherham. The security man watched us but didn't say anything. We hit a 'seam' of coke (at the bottom of the stack, left there years ago) and managed to get fourteen bags full. Sold the lot for £3 a bag and split the money. Arthur Scargill did not turn up at court today- case adjourned until next Wednesday. He could be in Pentonville over Christmas.

There has been a lot of trouble at Woolley Colliery, near Barnsley. Nineteen coppers were hurt in one day. The pickets there took the police by surprise and forty police ran across the fields like rabbits.

Blood-spatted miner and official picket Ralph Summerfield, following an attack by police using dogs near Woolley colliery. Ralph Summerfield/Yorkshire Miner

Friday, 5 October

Orders for today: Kiveton Park. 5 am but went out with the coke money and overlaid!

Monday, 8 October

Orders for today: Silverwood.

Went out with coke money and overlaid again.

Tuesday, 9 October

Kiveton Park. £3 petrol. 5 am.

Got to Kiveton OK and stood directly across from the pit entrance, a dangerous spot as there was a deep ditch nearby. Someone kept throwing crisp bags full of water at the police front line. The police were OK, thinking that it was funny – until they found out that it was not always water that the bags contained. Someone was urinating in them! After getting a direct hit they walked slowly away, arms outstretched, behind their lines. The cavalry appeared, totally disregarding the life and limb of any pickets who happened to be in their way. The only escape for me was to dive into the blinking ditch, getting soaked as a result.

Wednesday, 10 October

Orders for today: Kiveton and then back to Silverwood. Got to the same location again – opposite the pit entrance and near the blessed ditch. We must like getting into the thick of the action. Some comedian has brought a glove puppet, a bit like Sooty – taking the Michael out of Superintendent Nesbit who was asked by 'Sooty' if he was going to be taking any prisoners today. The Superintendent was not very amused since the cavalry made another charge at us. This time I lowered myself more carefully into the ditch and didn't get too wet. I waited until the cavalry had had their fun and went back to the pit yard. Made our way back to the car, then to Silverwood, some breakfast and home.

Thursday, 11 October

Destination Kiveton, 4 am, then fall back to Silverwood.

It's getting dangerous at Kiveton, picketing in the dark. We arrived on time and walked to the pit entrance but I kept well clear of that ditch! We mingled with the other pickets, about 200–300 were present. After about an hour of waiting the scabs went in from the bottom lane, entering the pit from the countryside, in the opposite direction of the village. After they had gone in Chief Super Nesbit, using a loudhailer, shouted 'BUGGER OFF HOME OR THE CAVALRY IS COMING OUT'. I'm getting fed up with this bloke. We kept a fair bit away from the pit entrance and that ditch but two minutes later the cavalry appeared from the pit gates (as promised), followed by dozens of police. Mind you, they did not charge out this morning, just trotted. We had no choice, so were forced up the road and into the village. I kept looking behind me. It was dark and you can't be too careful. When we got to the terraced houses, just before the village, the cavalry returned to their stables and the police took over. They wanted us to go home! But once we were in the village they left us alone. Went back to Silverwood. Couldn't get near the fire. We all bought a cig for ten pence. Hung around till the scabs went in, then I dropped the lads off home.

Friday, 12 October

Expected a good day today. Talks are continuing at ACAS. Wonder if a settlement might be reached. When we got to Brodsworth we parked in a field, away from the police and started walking towards the pit. Trouble started straight away. The cavalry came from behind so about a hundred of us were pushed down the road. When they were not looking a few bricks were thrown. It was an ideal battleground for us – small hedges and allotments. The village [Woodlands] was a few hundred yards away. Lost Bob Taylor and Daz so went with Shaun to look for our mates in the main body of pickets. We took advantage of a good opportunity to disturb the cavalry in the open field since they were thinly spread and not too many of them. With Shaun and Bob Wilson, I made for the cavalry (Shaun was a bit wary about joining in but I assured him that horses can not run through ploughed fields, but I don't know where I got that information from!), keeping a safe distance, near to the hedges. Joined up with thirty other pickets and we ran into the field and began attacking the cavalry with bricks and stones. We were not that brave so needed some ammo! They responded by charging us, so over the hedges we jumped. We attacked them again and once again retreated to safety, over the hedges. At the time of our third attack the scabs started going in via a convoy, all hell was let loose around the pit entrance. I went too far into the field to get the cavalry; but one of them in front of me charged at me, waving a truncheon. I let him get within camera distance and took a photograph and then threw a stone at him. I just managed to get away as he had been startled by the photograph, which gave me a few precious seconds to escape; but his mate outflanked me, galloping along the hedges, his truncheon swiping out at anything in his way. I dove into a hedge even though it was full of brambles but he got me on my left arm, when I was in mid-air. A fair old crack it was and very painful. Then, three vans full of police reinforcements wearing riot gear drove into the field. I climbed out of the hedge, tidied myself and, holding my injured arm, looked to my right and noticed 'Our Kid' [Bob Wilson] in action. He'd found a wooden pole, about eight foot long, and stuck it into the mud, pointing it in the

'The day we took the cavalry on and lost'. The 'X' marks the spot where Bruce 'got some truncheon' at Brodsworth on 12 October 1984. John Sturrock/Network

1984 "BATTLE OF BROOSWORTH" (DAY OF THE BRIGHTON BOMB) AND THE DAY I GOT SOME TRUNCHEON

'X' MARKS THE SPOT "THE DAY WE TOOK THE CAVALRY ON - AND LOST"

direction of the cavalry riding in his direction. Bloody Hell! he could have killed somebody. The cavalry were not interested – they stopped and retreated. What an action today – the cavalry beat back by a single picket!

I started walking back through the field towards the rest of the men, only to be met by the riot squad. I was watching, and taking photographs of six policemen who were truncheoning one picket to the ground. They stopped when the saw me with my camera. One of them, looking like Darth Vader from *Star Wars*, came for me out of nowhere. He meant business, shield and truncheon at the ready, shouting, 'COME HERE YOU BASTARD!' Holding my bad arm, I replied in a similar way: 'FUCK OFF!' I had a couple of small bricks in one hand and my camera in the other. I dropped the bricks and took his photograph and as he came for me I turned away but bumped into another policeman who was fighting with a picket. All three of us fell over a hedge. I managed to get up and walk away. The policeman wearing an ordinary uniform said to the riot policeman, 'Which one shall we nick?' The latter replied, 'Get that fat Bastard', referring to the poor old picket, so they left me and truncheoned the other miner who fell to the ground. I climbed on to the roof of a pigeon loft, struggling to do so, because of the pain from my injured arm. I could see about two hundred pickets surging across the field, coming to help us but the riot squad stopped them; then the main body of pickets fought back after the riot squad gave them a baton charge. A barrage of missiles went over that thick it was like a flock of starlings flying overhead. I got down from the pigeon loft and returned to the main body of pickets. Then the police charged all of us up the road and into the village. One of the riot squad forgot himself and carried on charging after his mates had stopped. He got kicked and beaten and his mates had to give him medical attention.

It's been an eventful day. I took off my T-shirt again as they might have recognised me on the way back to the car. I stuffed it down my vest. The police tried a new tactic, they put about a hundred men at a road junction or along the road, and then pick men out who they believed had caused trouble – but we are quick learners – you had to be in order to avoid the truncheon and get nicked this morning. How I managed to escape arrest I will never know. It was a good day for the miners.

Twelve arrests in hour of violence

ELEVEN police and several pickets were injured in fighting outside Brodsworth colliery, Doncaster.

Two of the police suffered head injuries and were detained overnight in Doncaster Royal Infirmary.

An estimated 3,500 pickets were confronted by about 1,500 police around dawn as three miners went in to work.

The trouble lasted for about an hour and 12 people were arrested.

Police tactics were criticised by Sheffield policewatch, whose observers said the use of 22 horses to chase pickets across a ploughed field triggered the violence.

Events culminated in re-

against pickets throwing missiles.

A statement claimed one observer saw police hitting arrested pickets as they were taken through police lines.

"If the police had not used horses to pursue pickets at a time when the picket was entirely peaceful, the whole morning's events would probably have remained calm," it said.

A police van on the M18 heading for Brodsworth had its windscreen smashed by a brick dropped from a bridge. No one was injured.

The NCB said the picket was the biggest mounted in the last ten days and it described it as very well

"The question has to be asked, who is doing the orchestrating?" it said.

South Yorkshire assistant chief constable Tony Clement said of the Police watch allegations: "I have heard this so often that it is becoming almost boring. We have on numerous occasions put our officers in a line across a road and just stood there and then the stoning has begun and we have reacted to that stoning.

"We do not put horses into a situation where people are just standing and shouting and demonstrating in that way. We will only use horses if we are under attack and that attack is usually by

I took the film in for processing but not a single shot turned out. It makes you think if my film had been tampered with.

Not much on telly tonight about the strike but somebody has tried to blow Mrs Thatcher and her Conservative Government up at Brighton today.

Saturday, 13 October
Went potato picking for a day, with my team. A welcome rest from the picket line. The last time I did this I

The 'hour of violence' at Brodsworth, as described in a local newspaper, 12 October 1984. Sheffield Star

126

was aged fourteen. The picking up points were either the *Queen's Hotel* or the Baths Hall, Rawmarsh. We felt a bit daft, us miners with a load of kids. The farmer collected us and we got into a horsebox which reminded me of 'Wild Mouse', a man-riding mail down 'Braithwell Two' development at Silverwood which used to go all over the place – people would have paid good money to experience that mail! When we got to our site we were designated as 'lifters' at £9 a day. We would be rich at this rate so got stuck in to the job. We lifted baskets of spuds and emptied them into the farm trailer which continually went round all the spud pickers. It was water off a duck's back for us. Come dinner time we happened to be in a field across from the *Marquis Hotel*, at Haugh. We went into the tap room. There were a few people inside. Some of them we knew, including a local who had moved up in life. I think he ought really to be a miner instead of being in the tap room. Anyway, Mr Zammito, the landlord, guessed who we were and what we were doing. I went to the bar and just had enough money for half a bitter for each of us but nothing spare, not even for a packet of crisps to share. Mr Zammito asked his son, Pablo, to go into the kitchen and and get some chips for us lads. I explained to Mr Zammito that we were OK and that we could not afford any chips but he told us that it was 'on the house.' I felt a lump in my throat. Someone came from the kitchen with a basket of chips for us to share. They were beautiful! As we were about to leave I thanked Mr Zammito for his hospitality and told him that after the strike I would return and buy him a drink (I did do this).

Monday, 15 October

Depart from Baggin at 3 30 am. Double 'un today – Brookhouse, then fall back to Kiveton Park. Arrived at the Beighton end of Brookhouse, having travelled down the Sheffield Parkway. Had a cup of tea in the Miners' Welfare, then set off up the road. Police on horses pushed us up, right to the top of the road (Swallownest end). Very quiet. Departed to Kiveton only to find that the scabs had gone in. No action today.

Tuesday, 16 October

Destination Shireoaks Colliery, Derbyshire, for 4 am. £4 petrol money. Tried all ways to get there but no chance of getting through. It was foggy, dark and there wasn't much time to play with, so we went down the A57 to Worksop. All the country lanes were blocked, as expected. Twenty police were blocking the A57. Pickets' cars were parked sensibly in lay-by's etc (we did not want our windscreens 'accidentally damaged' by the police) and then we set off walking. The police were not wearing identification numbers and the snatch squad were in their fluorescent jackets. Made our way back to the cars and, thankfully, they were OK and went back to Baggin for a cup of tea.

News report concerning the blockage of the Worksop–Sheffield road, 16 October 1984. It also includes reference to the latest NCB 'return to work' figures. Sheffield Star

Road-block picket foiled

16·10·84·

POLICE foiled a mass picket attempt yesterday at Shireoaks Colliery, near Worksop, where two men are working.

The main Worksop to Sheffield road was blocked for half an hour when about 60 cars were abandoned at the Yorkshire border and about 600 pickets tried to walk to the pit — but only 24 pickets reached the pit entrance.

Stones were thrown at police vehicles, but no one was hurt. One picket was arrested accused of obstruction.

A few miles away at Manton five miners reported for work in spite of the presence of about 60 pickets.

Seven pickets were arrested when scuffles broke out as police tried to stop them sitting in the road outside Rossington colliery, Doncaster.

Police said the men were trying to stop a vehicle carrying working miners from the pit.

But NUM officials said they were sitting in the road hours before any vehicles came out and trouble only flared when police used excessive force to move them.

A lone miner now working at Ireland Colliery at Staveley, North Derbyshire, has been "planted" by the Coal Board an NUM official said last night.

John Burrows, a Derbyshire NUM treasurer, said: "He is a member of the area salvage team and not a normal employee at Ireland Colliery.

"I am convinced he has been planted there by the Coal Board so they can say they have someone working at every pit in Derbyshire.

"The lads at Ireland are incensed by this and some of those who have not been picketing during the strike have started doing so."

The NCB was yesterday claiming a record 1,027 miners at work in Derbyshire, 55 up on the previous day with 11 new starters.

Wednesday, 17 October

Captain Bob gets some truncheon – twice! For doing nothing!

Silverwood this morning. Picked the lads up and parked in the pit car park, near the Garage. Walked into the pit entrance. As we got there Inspector Nesbit emerged from the yard, shouting, 'ONLY SIX PICKETS ALLOWED THIS MORNING' (and all the rest were to … 'bugger off'). We walked back to the car, escorted by the police to begin with. After they had left us a van full of police pulled up and Shaun responded by shouting, 'LET'S GO AND TURN THAT VAN OVER', as a joke, and gave them a load of verbal. Then, a police riot van drove up the hill, so we dispersed into the safety of the fields. Bob Taylor carried on walking down the road on his own. The van stopped, Bob did not look round, he just carried on walking. The next minute, a bobby jumped out of the vehicle and truncheoned Bob, striking him on the right shoulder and told him to 'FUCK OFF'. Owd Bob carried on walking down the road. Another van pulled up near him. Again, Bob did not look round, as he wasn't doing anything wrong. A bobby jumped out and truncheoned Bob yet again, hitting him on his back and shoulders. They had it in for Captain Bob today. Anyway, Bob stuck to his guns and got back to the car none the worse (apart from a few bruises) for his experience.

Thursday, 18 October

After a quiet week, we were sent, early morning, to Rossington Colliery, near Doncaster. They say you can't beat the system but we keep trying. The Government is trying to break the strike, especially in South Yorkshire, but after eight months there's probably only one or two men at work at each colliery in our area. There were about two thousand pickets at Rossington to begin with. We parked well away from the pit. We had to walk through fields etc to get to the pit gates. It was pitch dark. A hundred pickets charged about fifty riot police, shouting, 'WE'RE MINERS, WE'RE MINERS, WE'LL NEVER BE DEFEATED!' It lifted my heart, all them young lads charging. The police were terrified. Half an hour later 1500 to 2000 miners came marching down the road, a sight for sore eyes; and when a convoy of police came down the road they were attacked with stones and bricks. A police horsebox, as big as a double-decker bus, drove onto the causeway to try and deliberately run down a picket. He was lucky to escape with 'only' serious injury. During all this some pickets removed a man-hole cover in the main road. Police vans came speeding down the road, and one of them ran into the hole. The back doors opened and a copper fell out and the following police van hit him but he was only bruised and shaken. Someone had lit a fire in the road. The cavalry and riot squad turned out but no prisoners were taken.

Someone has a lot to answer for regarding this strike – especially Thatcher. To the Tories a scab is a hero.

Typical for rest of the morning: very severe hand-to-hand fighting. We went round the back streets in the village and saw the riot police and the pickets battling all over the place. We saw two miners, both in their twenties, one of them carrying a riot shield and fires were burning all over. Police were jumping on miners, pickets were ambushing the police etc. We never got back to the pit entrance this morning and I wasn't bothered as we picketed safely, in numbers, well back up the road. When we were making our way back to the car we bumped into small groups of pickets doing the same. We got there via fields etc. Police won't follow us over countryside, especially in the dark.

Friday, 19 October

Orders for today: Brodsworth Colliery.

Overlaid, recovering from yesterday. Deputies have voted by 82% majority in favour of strike action.

Monday, 22 October

Silverwood, then Thurcroft Colliery.

Overlaid, had a day off

Tuesday, 23 October

Decided to join mass picket at Silverwood. All the South Yorkshire area picketing Silverwood but when we got there there were only about 300 pickets. On telly it stated about 1500! Someone has triple vision. Very quiet today, mind you, we were surrounded by cavalry and riot squad, with the snatch squads also there. Went to the Baggin after scabs went in, had some eggs and beans – we're beginning to look like eggs and beans.

Wednesday, 24 October

Yorkshire Main, Edlington, near Doncaster.

Overlaid. Saw events on telly later – 3,000 pickets?

Thatcher is 'pulling the strings;, according to this cartoon by Vollans in a strike issue of the Yorkshire Miner. Yorkshire Miner

Thursday, 25 October

Orders: Silverwood, then Kiveton Park Colliery. Had some 'Zulu' at Kiveton: pushing and shoving at the end of our stint. Pickets shouted, 'DON'T GO! MAKE THEM STAND HERE AND EARN THEIR MONEY'. Inspector Nesbit told us that if we did not move away now the cavalry would arrive. He was not taking any prisoners again this morning. We didn't move and they did take prisoners! Just across from the pit entrance is a great ditch, half full of water. The cavalry appeared and I jumped into the ditch, getting absolutely soaked. The cavalry charged up the hill. Two nice policemen offered to help me out of the ditch but I declined – as fed up and wet as I was, I did not like the idea of being helped out and then arrested – though the two officers did seem sincere.

This flying picket job is getting harder – I could do with a rest sometime soon!

This morning, when we got to the front line, a miner called Sam Hackleton, a Cortonwood lad, was there. A picket said to a front line policeman, 'God you are ugly, you are uglier than Sam 'Hack'. The bobby smiled. The next moment, a miner standing next to the bobby shouted Bob Hackleton to come over. 'Hack' must have been a good 22 stone and a face like an ex-boxer or wrestler. When he saw him the bobby soon stopped smiling!

Courts are sequestering NUM funds – owt that they can get their hands on. My wife, Gay, comes back from her mother's tomorrow (London). Her uncle Jim, from Hertfordshire (who serves in the Hertfordshire Constabulary) is coming back for some more action next week, in Derbyshire.

Friday, 26 October
Exactly as yesterday: Kiveton and Silverwood, £3 petrol money. At Kiveton there were about 2,000 pickets and loads of police. Same old story – not enough of us, you can't say 'Boo!' or you are arrested. Went to Silverwood later, parking at the *Cavalier*, and then walked it down to the pit. Had only been there about ten minutes when the scabs went in. There were some women from NALGO (Sheffield) on the picket line, supporting the miners.

Monday, 29 October
Silverwood. All quiet. Stood around the fire and had a nice cup of tea. Did our usual 5–6 hour stint. I may have a few days off next week.

Tuesday, 30 October
Silverwood again: nice and quiet. Stood around the fire. Bought *a* cig from the tea hut. It used to open when the pit was working, selling cigs, tea etc for miners starting or finishing their shift. The man and his wife sold cigarettes in ones, which was a blessing for us as we had so little money. The hut stood directly across from the pit lamproom. Went back to the Baggin for some snap.

Wednesday, 31 October
Silverwood, early morning. When we arrived, police were playing football in the pit yard. Pickets had a fire going in an old oil drum but all the wood that was available was damp, so smoke was drifting into the pit yard, choking the 'players'. Superintendent Nesbit came out and instructed us to put the fire out, followed by some of his men, carrying buckets of water. Dave Vickers (a Silverwood pit bottom loco driver) was next to the fire. The police poured water onto the fire, causing even more smoke. The wind direction sent it into the pit yard rather then towards the pickets. There was a solution: Nesbit agreed not to pour anymore water and we could still have our fire.

VIII

A Bleak Midwinter and a Not So Happy Christmas

November/December 1984

'… we hardly had any coal,
we're burning old shoes..'

This witty Christmas cartoon/card by TC Bray shows that there was still a sense of humour around despite the prospect of a hard winter.

EDITOR'S SUMMARY

The onset of winter and declining family finances meant that there was not much festive cheer in the homes of striking miners. High Court injunctions and Price Waterhouse continued to attempt to undermine the finances of an increasingly defiant National Union of Minerworkers. The Government itself, via the DHSS, announced a further £1 reduction from benefits paid to striking miners on 21 November. Non-existent strike pay was already deducted. On the same day the NCB claimed that 5,952 men had gone back in a single week, the number of working miners now exceeding 62,000. However, determination was as strong as ever in South Yorkshire. On 9 November a mass picket assembled at Cortonwood to 'greet' a lone scab and on the previous day some 6,000 miners and supporters attended a mass rally in Sheffield.

Bruce swallowed his pride and obtained a complimentary jumper, very handy for cold mornings when picketing but the old battlebus was just about knackered. A bit of logging in the woods was an essential activity when there was little or no coal to heat water and, at the very least, keep a young family warm. And yet picketing somehow continued, mainly on the Silverwood 'day-shift' but also to nearby pits, including Thurcroft, Manvers, Brookhouse and Kilnhurst. A visit to Dinnington on 6 December was significant for kid brother Bob – now a 'wanted man' – who was snatched from Bruce's arms by eagle-eyed policemen. Despite all the misery, Christmas came as a welcome relief and welcome rest, children did receive a few presents and the generosity of friends and family (despite an odd joke) was appreciated.

The now-famous Alamo picket in the depth of winter. Arthur Wakefield

A few working miners can be seen in the distance, most pickets, both men and women, kept at a safe distance by the police. However, a lone picket is just visible, having just popped out of the 'tea hut', probably shouting 'SCAB!'

THE DIARY
Friday, 2 November

Silverwood, on day shift again. Watched the scabs go in, We decided to go down to the Rotherham Assembly Rooms where there was clothing donated by Germany and other European countries. We swallowed our pride and went to see what was available. I got a lovely thick, woollen jumper, well-made and warm – they know how to make good quality clothing in Germany. Shaun was looking at all the clothes on the rails. I told him that *Calendar* was filming him for the tea time news. He dropped what he was holding as though they were hot bricks and shot off. It is embarrassing and it hurts your pride, accepting 'cast-offs' but we badly needed warm clothing for picketing during the winter months. Something that gives you freedom of movement and not too heavy and cumbersome is ideal – especially for picket duty.

Went home 're-clothed', at teatime. I went with Arthur Brasher and another Kilnhurst miner to pick coal. We went by the side of the low bridge at Kilnhurst, near to the pit. Tried some of

Silverwood striking miners and their families picketing across from the colliery entrance.
Bob Taylor

the 'coal' over the weekend. It's a good job I only had a couple of sacks since the stuff just did not burn.

Monday, 5 November

Silverwood. Days. It's getting boring now, just picketing outside your own pit. Stood outside the pit gates, shouting at the scabs when they went in to work, then we go home. Too cold to do anything else anyway. We got a bag of smokeless fuel from Rotherham Council – one bag a week, payable after the strike ends, and we only get it as we have got young children. Thought I would invest in a bow saw blade, £1.25 from B & Q. I've already got the saw. No coal, no money. Set off for the nearest wood, found a small one, across the road from Lynskey's excavations at Kilnhurst. Three days I was at it, leaving a wood which had no trees in the middle of it, and had a pile of logs as high as myself. When I'd done I got the fire going, using a few old shoes as fire-lighters and got a good fire going. I think we will need a new Parkray soon, though, but it still gets the house and the water warm.

134

The rest of the month:

November was a quiet month for picketing, usual routine of getting to Silverwood in the morning, though there were a few occasions when we went to Kilnhurst pit. The situation there is definitely that they have their own way, or we do. When the scabs went in, from the main road by the side of the canal, not much effort was made to stop them but if they came the other way, via Kilnhurst Road, and under the low bridge, well, they weren't thick. Anyway, I think the NUM weren't too worried about Kilnhurst.

One morning on picket duty at Kilnhurst stands out. At 1 am we set off, and had not far to travel, just down the road. We thought that there might be some fun as the police presence was not too great, although we did not know what support they might have had in the pit yard. Police in Transit vans were patrolling the road, from the low bridge, round the bend, where the pit entrance is and down Glasshouse Lane. We were on the bridge and there was miles of countryside on either side of us – and unlimited supplies of 'ammo' at our feet (railway

Here, we have a good view of Silverwood colliery, pickets and the tarpaulin-covered picket shelter.

ballast). When it was all dark and quiet the police vans would cruise up, slowly and then stop a good fifty yards from us; they couldn't see us but they were aware we were there. They would not come any closer and we never saw any riot police.

A few days later when picketing in daylight hours, dozens of police went by us but we couldn't believe it as the police totally ignored us. They just marched past us and raided the scrapyard, just up from the pit, as the man there was alleged to be dealing in stolen motors, breaking them for parts. On this day they thought more about cars than scabs.

Thursday, 6 December
Silverwood, 3 am, then Thurcroft and Dinnington pits.

Didn't stop at Silverwood but went on to Thurcroft. It was quiet, about 300 pickets there. All of us stood on some grass, nowhere near the pit gates. The police nicked one young miner. He wore a full-face black balaclava, with slits for his eyes and mouth. We were surrounded by the police. They had got us where they wanted: penned in! They reached in and arrested another young miner for no reason. There were women among us, too. The police just arrested who they wanted, ignoring cries of dismay from a woman whose son had been snatched. We (my crew) decided to move on.

Went on to Dinnington Colliery. There were about 150 of us there and we were able to stand on ground dead opposite the pit entrance. It was fairly quiet. There were just ordinary police in front of us, but, suddenly, the snatch squad came out – big bastards, all well over six-foot tall, wearing fluorescent jackets but with no numbers. We had only been facing them for five minutes when one of them reached out and grabbed Bob Wilson. He pulled himself back into the crowd of miners but they still hung on to him but would not come into the crowd. I put my arm around his and wrapped my other arm around a lampost. For a few minutes Bob was playing tug-of-war – police on one side and me and him on the other; then one of the snatch squad leant over and grabbed my nose, twisted it between his fingers. It was so painful that I let go of Bob. This was about 6. 30 am. They took him into the pit yard, two big bastards, one either side of him. He was taken round the back and told to stop struggling with a warning of, 'Nobody can see us now … we can knock shit out of you!' At least they gave him an option so Bob decided to 'go quietly'. He finished up being fined £400 but I suppose it could have been much worse. The NUM paid the fine (see 14 December, below).

Friday, 7 December
Manvers this morning, 5.30.

About 300 pickets turned out. It was quiet, no trouble.

Attended Doncaster Court this morning. My brother, Bob Wilson was freed on bail at 1.15 pm but he had been held in custody for 33 hours! It turned out that the motorbike bobby that Bob had jumped out on, and said Boo! was at Dinnington yesterday and had pointed Bob out to the snatch squad. Bob was charged with a right shopping list of 'crimes': assault, criminal damage, GBH etc etc and all he had done was scare a copper riding his bike. Bob thinks he was lucky to escape the charge of attempted murder!

Monday, 10 December
Shirebrook, North Derbyshire.

Told to expect roadblocks. Set off at 11 pm and arrived at midnight. Supped tea and played cards all night and started picketing from 4.45 am. Scouse police were on duty. Everything was OK until the Notts police arrived. Then the scabs arrived, six or seven coach loads of them, followed by a few cars. Out of the 800 men employed at the pit I reckon about 600 are now going in to work. The official picket managed to turn the deputies back. An under manager was at the pit gates, trying to coax them in. Pickets had been successful in turning the deputies back for the last few weeks. There were at the pit top, arguing about being paid only a day-wage and how cold the weather was! Got home at 7 am.

Tuesday, 11 December
Silverwood for 4 am.

We're going to have a lay-in, though, so got there for 9 am. We had missed a mass picket, at 4.30 am. I need an engine and gearbox fitted on the car.

Wednesday, 12 December
Flyers to Brookhouse for 9 am. Scabs came out at 10.20 am.

I had to go to court. A Silverwood scab stood next to me. I did not know who he was at first, until the usher called out his name. My case was adjourned until 27 February 1985.

On telly tonight it was stated that 'the first coal produced in Yorkshire' had taken place – at Manton Colliery, though Manton is near Worksop, Nottinghamshire, though it is part of the NCB Yorkshire Area.

Thursday, 13 December
Instructions to report to Baggin for 5 am, then to go flying but overlaid. Got to the pit at 11 am, but in time to catch the scabs. Called to the Baggin for some dinner.

Manton deputies came out today. They said that they came out because of 'police intimidation'. When the scabs went in the pickets had a shove and the coppers waded into them, dishing out some hammer. the deputies witnessed this, so went home.

One of the Silverwood scabs has made nine statements against our pickets who are expecting a knock at their doors at any time. Arthur Critchlow is top of their list. Arthur is a 'front-liner' like ourselves. He was arrested at Orgreave in June and, with others, was charged with 'Riot' etc which carried a Life Sentence! Arthur was truncheoned at Orgreave and unbelievable bail conditions were imposed on him – he could not leave his house and spent some time in Armley Jail after being arrested.

The case against the NUM appointing a receiver has been adjourned until a full hearing in March 1985.

Bob Wilson is up at Doncaster Court tomorrow, 14 December.

Friday, 14 December
The following statement, supplied on behalf of Mr Robert Wilson, concerned his whereabouts on 13 September 1984 when he was charged with various offences that took place at Yorkshire Main Colliery during a mass picket. He was accused of knocking a police motorcyclist off his bike, among other things. The charges were serious – he might not be able to go to the pub for a while. He was caught at a later date by the snatch squad at Dinnington Colliery. I used a bit of discretion in my statement, playing them at their own game, and had a bit of 'amnesia' as well.

A strong police presence is evident from this photograph of the picket line at Silverwood colliery in the winter of 1984. The NUM building can be seen on the right of the photograph.

My Statement

On Thursday 13 September 1984 I, Bruce Wilson, set off to pick up my regular crew members for picket duty. We would picket our own pit, Silverwood Colliery. At 1 am I picked up Mr Robert Wilson first as he lived closest to me. After picking the rest of the lads up we arrived at Silverwood Colliery about 3 am. Apart from myself, there were R. Wilson, Robert Taylor, Darren Goulty and Shaun Bisby. We usually did a stint of 5 or 6 hours.

That morning, the two working miners went in at about 4 am. There was a push, something went on at the front line and a miner was arrested. His name was Craig Dimbleby. Mr Dimbleby was taken into the pit yard by the police. Our NUM Treasurer, Mr Eric Cassidy, one of the six official pickets allowed, exchanged a few words with the officer in charge and Mr Dimbleby was released. Mr Dimbleby remembers Mr R. Wilson well, because he was one of the first miners he spoke to after his release. We stopped at Silverwood until about about 8 am. Then I dropped the lads off at their houses. We did not go anywhere else, as our Union only gave me £2 petrol money. My car is a Triumph 2500 TC and only does about 23 miles to the gallon. My home is about five miles from the pit. We stopped flying to other areas (Notts, Derbyshire etc) in late August so as to concentrate on picketing our own pit, Silverwood. The NUM verify us as being present at Silverwood on that morning. I can get a copy of their records for obvious reasons (their records show that we signed a form to collect our £1 picket money on that morning).

Yours sincerely
Bruce Wilson

The first part of the letter is entirely true, Craig getting nicked etc, but our morning's orders were in fact to fly to Yorkshire Main after the scabs had gone in at Silverwood. All is fair in love and war (they say).

My statement did not work. Our kid got arrested and was fined £400. The NUM paid the fine for him. The policeman on the motorbike had a good memory!

Another photograph showing police on duty at Silverwood. The lamp room entrance can be seen on the middle, right of the photograph.

Let's make it a Happy Christmas (and a confident New Year) in the pit villages.

The great majority of miners are still on strike. They and their families are desperately poor.

A recent report from the Dawdon Miners Distress Centre, Co. Durham says that 30% of the striking miners are destitute. It reports:

"Our biggest problem at the moment is trying to ensure that our children are dressed and have shoes on their feet".

The report ends: "I cannot of course begin to tell you of the desolation we all feel, especially when we are talking about people who are basically honest, who have paid their taxes and debts to this society and who, in any circumstances, are honest citizens and by their nature, proud and caring parents."

The distress of the miners and their families has not daunted their fighting spirit. They are as determined as ever to save their communities, their jobs and our coal.

They have a right to a good Christmas.

This is an urgent appeal for a huge Christmas bonus for the striking miners and their families. A little money goes a long way.

£300 will provide a Christmas dinner for 200.

£50 will finance a Christmas party in a miners welfare hall.

£10 will buy a turkey.

£2 will fill a stocking for a miners child.

If all who want to do something to help the coal mining communities give some money to this fund, we can ensure for the communities a happy Christmas and a confident New Year.

This appeal has raised £200,000 so far. Help us make it half a million!

This appeal is supported by over 6,000 people including:

Larry Adler
Dame Peggy Ashcroft
Aswad
Tony Benn MP
Alan Bleasdale
Anthony Booth
Jackie Charlton
Julie Christie
Brian Clough
Billy Connolly
Judi Dench
Clive Dunn
Dafydd Elis Thomas MP
Sir Moses and Lady Finlay
The Flying Pickets
Paul Foot
John Fowles
Tony Galvin, Spurs
Brian Glover
Green of Scritti Politsi
Sheila Hancock
Roy Hattersley MP
Denis Healey MP
Bishop Trevor Huddleston
Simon Hughes MP
Glenda Jackson
Jack Jones
Miriam Karlin
Ben Kingsley
Glenys Kinnock
Neil Kinnock MP
Ken Livingstone
Kenny Lynch
Malcolm MacLaren
Rik Mayall
George Melly
Spike Milligan
Bel Mooney
John Mortimer QC
Pat Nevin, Chelsea
Michael Palin
Molly Parkin
Pat Phoenix
Nigel Planer
Prunella Scales
Alan Sillitoe
Jon Snow
Janet Suzman
John Thaw
Pete Townshend
UB40
Julie Walters
Fay Weldon
Colin Welland
Paul Weller,
Prof Raymond Williams
David Yip
Susannah York

To Miners Families Christmas Appeal c/o 14 Whittlesley Street, London SE1 8SL.

I/We enclose a donation of £_____ for the Miners Families Christmas Appeal (Cheque/PO made out to 'Miners Families Christmas Appeal').

To save costs, no receipt will be sent unless requested. (Tick below)

Please send receipt ☐

NAME

ADDRESS

Postcode

ORGANISATION (if any)

There was a great deal of public support for the miners as Christmas approached, as can be seen by this notice which also lists well known people from politics, entertainment, sport and the church who were pleased to add their names to the Miners' Families Appeal.

There are now about 18 men going in to work at Silverwood Colliery. One of them wrote to the NUM asking to rejoin the strike; another thinks that nobody knows that he is working and had the cheek to turn up for a strike hamper the other day. Another scab did the same.

Christmas

Just picketed our own pit, Silverwood, but also had 'excursions' to Kilnhurst and Treeton collieries. Stopped picketing one week before Christmas and then had nearly two weeks off.

Gay's mum sent us a food parcel, containing a few things that we could not otherwise afford. The kids did not do too bad as we took them on a round of Christmas parties, one at the Baggin, one at the Cricket Club (Rawmarsh) and a couple of others; and then there were their school parties. They either got some money or a little present.

Gordon, one of my younger brothers, sent us a Christmas card but when I opened it he had sellotaped a tea bag inside! 'Have a drink on me' was his motto! Any other time and we would have found it funny but it's a hard time for us, so it was not really a good time for him to be a

Silverwood miners and their families show patience and support when picketing at Silverwood colliery.

A group of police stand in front of a board listing the names of 'scabs' but after a few minutes the 'offending' item is carried away (opposite). One of the pickets (finger in ear) is Arthur Critchlow who faced serious charges after Orgreave.

comedian: we hardly had any coal, were burning old shoes, in fact anything that would give off a bit of heat and provide us with warm water. Mind you, he bought me a few pints over Christmas. He thought the tea bag 'gift' really funny.

A neighbour brought round a bag of apples and oranges. I thanked him and Gay looked inside the bag – but the oranges were covered in mould and the apples were windfalls. I waited until it was dark and disposed the contents of the bag into the dustbin. Well, it's the thought that counts, and we were not that desperate.

We did not go without as family and friends helped us out and did the rounds of kids' Christmas parties. *The Fighting Cocks* at Rawmarsh had a party for kids and they all got presents. Then we went to the Baggin and got a present and some money. Then we took them to the Titanic [WMC]. Gay bought a second-hand rocking horse for our Suzanne, for £2. Our Rick got a boxing punch bag from Gay's catalogue and woke up Christmas morning knocking

seven bells out of it. Grandparents also bought them presents so the kids had a decent Christmas in the circumstances.

Went out with Gay a couple of times over Christmas. On Boxing day we had a good night out. Sometime ago my grandmother gave me some sets of 1981 and 1982 coins of Great Britain which went towards the evening.

We enjoyed a nice little Christmas-day dinner. Gay bought a cheap 'Bernard Matthews' turkey breast joint and we pulled a cracker and put a hat on!

It was nice to have a rest from the picket line over Christmas and the New Year. My brother, Gordon and myself had many a laugh over his 'tea bag' gift, though at the time we did not have two half-pennies to rub together and hardly any fuel. MARGARET THATCHER IS THROWING EVERYTHING SHE'D GOT AT US, INCLUDING THE KITCHEN SINK.

IX
Snowmen at Cortonwood
January/February 1985

'Crash, bang, wallop ...'

Cortonwood men playing cards inside the Alamo picket hut, 29 January 1985. Parry/Brian Elliott

EDITOR'S SUMMARY

The dates of Bruce's diary entries become less precise towards the end of the strike, though it is clear that there was no let up in picketing. The battlebus finally succumbed to old age and wear and tear, broken up for scrap, and replaced by an old Austin Maxi. Bruce and his team now concentrated their efforts on Cortonwood and a couple of now legendary 'snowmen' incidents are reported at first hand. The village of Brampton where Cortonwood pit was located appears to have been in a state of siege during this period, not only with front line clashes but chases through the main and side streets and on the colliery lane. The Alamo picket hut lived up to its name and the village was a focus for national and international media attention.

It must have felt disheartening when more miners were reported, albeit by the never to be trusted NCB, to be back at work. On 25 February it was claimed that a further 3,807 miners had returned, the highest Monday figure so far. There was now an approximate balance of numbers between striking and working miners.

Striking miners continued to be arrested for a wide range of alleged offences. By 15 February the total arrest figure surpassed 9,500 for England and Wales.

Prospects for a negotiated agreement were bleak. Talks between the executive committee of the NUM and the NCB broke down on 29 January and a document produced by Thatcher and Walker and eventually scrutinised by the TUC was rejected.

THE DIARY
January
My old battlebus – the mobile picket machine – has had it. Parked her on my mother's drive, 220 Kilnhurst Road, Rawmarsh and had to break her up. It took me two days. All I used were spanners, a hacksaw, hammer and chisels. Completely stripped her down, so all that was left was the engine and gearbox. Gave them to 'Razzer' (a Silverwood lad) for scrap. He came round and we loaded them by hand into a small trailer. The price of scrap was high, £60 a ton. I weighed the old battlebus in for £80, alloy wheels, alloy cylinder head, copper radiator plus other bits and bobs. Our kid, Gordon, who was not a miner, owned a pickup and transported the scrap for me. Mrs Ridgeway, who lives next door, a nice lady, came out one day and said that she knew about my circumstances but also said that she would report me to the council if I did that sort of work again – and she meant it.

Thursday, 3 January
Got a 'new' car – an old Austin Maxi 1750, for £30. I borrowed the money to buy it, took it to the Union, showed them the receipt and they gave me £30 back – and even taxed it for me. It is tested until June 1985.

Monday, 7 – Friday 11 January
Silverwood for 10.30 am. Chief Superintendent Nesbit went around the car park, checking to see if we were all legal.

The NCB reckon that a thousand men went back to work this week.

Monday, 14 January
Silverwood, 4.30 am. Overlaid for the morning shift, so went on 'afternoons'. Paul Willis, a Silverwood miner (electrician) was nicked by the police outside the tea hut. The police had deliberately parked a van by the hut, stopping us getting in or out. They don't like us miners

Many women from mining communities provided tremendous support to striking miners. Here we can see an informal group of women and children sat on the grass bank opposite Silverwood colliery, the pit baths in the background.

Women express their feelings when working miners pass through the Silverwood pit entrance, police in the background.

A police Transit van, strategically parked in front of the 'Tea Hut' opposite Silverwood pit, makes access to this important facility very awkward for the picketing miners, 14 January 1985.

A determined but peaceful picket line on a cold January morning, standing opposite Silverwood colliery. The NUM branch office is on the left of the photograph.

One of the last mass pickets at Cortonwood is captured on this dramatic photograph which includes a number of Silverwood men, including Bruce and some of his crew. Note the television cameraman on the upper right of the photograph, using steps to assist his viewpoint.

The small arrowed figure is believed to be Silverwood miner Bill Robson, a drift engine mail driver who appears to have been snatched from the crowd.

having any 'luxuries' in life. The police have got it into their heads that the miners are holding the country to ransom, and should not be allowed to get away with it; their job is to uphold the law, not to be used politically as strike breakers.

Tuesday, 15 January
Silverwood, 4.30 am. Got to the *Reresby* pub at 5 am. Roadblocks on again. Went flying to Kiveton but missed them going in. Got there too late. The weather has been very cold, snowing all the time, a big freeze since Christmas. Some Doncaster working miners are taking our union leaders – Arthur Scargill, Mick McGahey and Peter Heathfield – to court, for 'organising all these mass pickets'. If they win it will mean just six pickets at each pit. The Government is trying all sorts of tactics to get us down. The NCB reports that 1300 men went back to work today. I'm sure they pull the numbers out of a hat! Anyway, it still leaves 135,000 still on strike!

Cortonwood Colliery (Brampton): 'The Alamo' (picket hut)
Chief Superintendent Nesbit: somebody remove that snowman!

Got there early. There was a fair covering of snow on the ground and it was cold and misty. Just stood there on the picket line, pickets and police both blocking the road. We were facing each other. Noticed that someone had built a snowman round a concrete bollard. Some miners started shouting at the police lines: 'ARE YOU TAKING PRISONERS TODAY SUPERINTENDENT NESBIT?' I don't think he likes personal comments being made to him. He instructed his officers to flatten the snowman but they appeared to look the other way so he got in a new Range Rover, revs it up and sets off straight at the offending snowman. Crash, bang, wallop – Mr Nesbit did not know about the concrete bollard in the middle!

It was quiet the rest of the day. One Range Rover written off. Bet someone will be paying for that and it could be us miners.

The next day at Cortonwood
Got there early morning. Pickets formed a front line by daylight. Shouts of 'ARE YOU TAKING PRISONERS, MR NESBIT?' and 'ARE YOU COMING OUT MR NESBIT?' were made, along with, 'THERE'S A SNOWMAN OUT HERE' I don't think Mr Nesbit will stand for this when, suddenly, to a shout of 'ZULU!' we all charged forward in one big push. I was caught at the front. Some lads next to me got lifted but apart from this the police were easy-going this morning. The police decided on new orders to keep the road clear from now on.

February [some actual dates not recorded]
As the days moved on things got bad at Cortonwood. The police were getting nasty. Day in and day out the riot squad went into action, keeping us all away from the pit entrance.

Went to Cortonwood early in the morning. Police are giving miners a rough time: things have changed here for the worst – the riot squad is continually chasing us through the streets. It came on the news that petrol bombs were being thrown at the police but this was not true. I saw some miners, standing next to me, throwing milk bottles at the police lines and warning them that if they don't stop their violence then the bottles will have petrol in them next time. They had carried them in crates from the corner shop. What do the police expect when we keep getting battered and hospitalised? We can't help doing some retaliation. It's getting nasty at Cortonwood on these dark mornings. This morning I was chased up the High Street. The police were jumping over walls. No questions were asked – you were truncheoned into submission or unconsciousness, then arrested. I saw one old man come out of his front door

– it was dark and early morning, and he had his donkey jacket on – when three riot police jumped over the small wall at the front of his house and knocked seven bells out of him – straight in with their truncheons, no kidding. His donkey jacket had a luminous patch on the back – he was a council worker, poor lad! Just imagine coming out of your front door, locking it, turning around and then being attacked by three men in black, using truncheons. The man was only on his way to work but finished up going to hospital instead. All morning the police ran riot through the streets of Brampton.

February [no date]

Arrived at Cortonwood this morning. It was cold and damp. Mr Nesbit wants the road clear. The police march out and form ranks across the road. There were loads of pickets today. I was on the front line but back a bit compared with last time. then it happened: a shout of 'ZULU!' and everybody surged forward. Had a good push. A few lads at the front got snatched by the police who then formed two lines and cleared the road. A miner with a sense of humour managed to built a small snowman, maybe from cotton wool. I was on the banking, watching, and, with my camera on me, it was a good opportunity to take a picture. The miner marched up and down, shouting for Mr Nesbit to come out and remove the 'offending' snowman: 'ARREST THAT SNOWMAN! ARREST THAT SNOWMAN!' he shouted. Police arrested the picket, ordered to by Mr

This series of photographs, taken from Bruce Wilson's camera, in February 1985, illustrates the 'artificial snowman' incident at Cortonwood. In the first two images we can see the picket, with arms raised, displaying the small 'offending' snowman, placed on the road by his feet; then, as he gains applause and shouts of encouragement and laughter from the men, he begins a short mock march in the middle of the road; but finally he is arrested/moved on, by the police, for blocking the highway.

Nesbit. I'm sure they were smiling when they took him away. I wonder what he will be charged with? Police seem to be OK so long as the road is kept clear. Captain Bob Taylor asked me a question: 'Na then, Bruce, when we have these pushes and Zulus, what would we do if we broke through?' It set me thinking did that one!

February [no date]

Silverwood for 4 am. Stayed for an hour then went flying to Cortonwood. Parked the car, up the lane, on a back street, near the working men's club. Walked down to the picket line and they were ready for action. When we got to the pit entrance some of the pickets had dragged a massive grass roller off the cricket pitch and were pushing it down the road, towards the police lines. I just stood there, watching, with Bob Taylor. The police front line just parted ranks. It was ever so funny, done so calmly. When the roller went through they just closed ranks again. Bet the police are fed up with clearing all the mess up when we have gone home.

Coal being moved by 'scab' drivers, from Silverwood colliery, amid a strong police presence.

February [no date]

Destination this morning Cortonwood. Arrived early, in pitch dark, a mass picket again. It's misty and cold. Made our way to the front line. The police want the road clear. We did not get near the pit entrance and neither did anyone else. The riot squad chased us up the road, all dressed in black, carrying shields and truncheons drawn. I turned to the left, into the housing estate. When I looked behind me whilst still running I could not see them but you could here them chasing you, mingling with the dark. I jumped over garden wall after garden wall, with other pickets. We managed to get well away from the pit but constantly looking around us. They arrested 'Tiger' this morning, two riot police dragging him away. Tiger is a Kilnhurst lad who lived in the 'concrete canyon' at Rawmarsh, near me. His photograph was on the front page of my newspaper the next day ['Tiger' was killed in a man-riding accident at Kilnhurst not long after the strike, jumping off the paddy when it was still moving, at the end of his shift.]

David Roper, a Silverwood striking miner, had a narrow escape when he was buried when digging for coal. He was rescued by the fire brigade and thanked them afterwards. This photograph was taken from the pit car park.

Another view showing lorries conveying coal from Silverwood colliery during the latter stages of the strike, with pickets looking on.

February [no date]

Flying to Cortonwood. Picked the lads up and made our way to Brampton. There were a few hundred miners today. Looks like this over the last few weeks. Everything is concentrated on the Alamo. We are flyers – Silverwood is safe enough as it has got its regular pickets. I got right to the front line. I fell again. Only been stood there a few minutes when up went the cry 'ZULU!' and we all pushed at the police front lines. A bobby just in front of me grabbed me by the shoulder, then wrapped his arm around mine. 'Got you!' he said. I pulled my arm out of his grip, elbowing him at the same time and managed to get away. The same bobby grabbed Bill Robson, a Silverwood man and passed him back towards his police mates, arrested. I mingled with the pickets. How I got away I don't know. Not too bad a morning, just a few arrests but I wasn't one of them.

Wednesday, 27 February

Had to go to court today, at Barnsley. Bill Robson had named me as a witness for him, following his arrest at Cortonwood. I couldn't see the point as I already knew what the outcome would be. Anyway, I picked Bill up. He was the engine driver at the top of 3's drift, and was also a barber by trade. He used to cut men's hair down the pit for some extra cash. He would sit you on an old box and give you short back and sides. We went to King Arthur's castle [NUM headquarters] first, to see a solicitor, and to get some expense money, petrol money for me. Then we went to Barnsley Court House. It was a waste of time. Bill got fined and I got a day out.

February [no date]

Silverwood, 4 am. Scabs went in, they are walking in now, from the pithead baths across the road. I could see some of their faces. Every pit has its weak men. There seemed a lot but maybe 15 or 20, but that's small compared to the size of the total workforce of approaching a thousand. One chap went in, walking from the pithead baths and across the road. Dave and some other lads recognised him and shouted his name just as he got into the pit yard, saying, 'What the fuck are tha doing? We've seen you!' He turned around and came out and joined the lads, explaining that he was just wanting to see who was going in. I don't think he realises how lucky he was but he made the right decision.

X

Return to Work and Redundancy and the Last Shift

March 1985–March 1988

'Immediately, a lump came in my throat.'

The great march back to work: Silverwood men and their Union banner arrive in the pit yard, 5 March 1985.

EDITOR'S SUMMARY[1]

Bruce provides us with some details of the end of the strike and the symbolic march back to work. He had a court appearance on his mind and must have felt both emotionally drained and dreadfully disappointed. But there is no doubt, like so many other striking miners, he was proud of the 'against the odds' fight against the NCB and Margaret Thatcher's unpopular government.

The tide of opinion towards a return to work *without an agreement* began via a few hectic days, beginning on Friday, 1 March when NUM areas in Durham, Lancashire and South Wales voted in favour. Scotland's vote was 'conditional' on an amnesty for sacked miners. On Saturday afternoon, 2 March, a meeting by the Yorkshire Area resulted in vote by a majority of just 4, in favour of the strike continuing; but, the day after, a special NUM delegate conference in London, held at the TUC headquarters, resulted in a 98–91 vote favouring a return to work. A Yorkshire resolution for an amnesty for sacked miners was defeated 91–98 at the delegate meeting. On Monday 4 March the Yorkshire Area Council meeting resulted in a recommendation of a return to work on Tuesday, 5 March, marching behind branch banners. Locally, at Silverwood, the branch voted that their march back would commence at 8 am, from the Baggin (Silverwood Miners' Welfare), on the agreed date.

Matters were by no means clear cut – not surprising given the flurry of national, regional and local meetings – and the feelings of the men after the year-long dispute, particularly in regard to sacked and jailed miners. The Silverwood men arrived at the pit gates at about 8.40 am but four Armthorpe (Markham Main) miners were present. The Armthorpe men were asked to remove their picket whilst the Silverwood branch executive could talk to the pit manager about the Silverwood miners who had been dismissed during the dispute. Similar events occurred at other Yorkshire pits when miners refused to cross the picket lines of Kent miners. The first actual day back at work, Wednesday 6 March, resulted in compulsory health and safety training and Bruce describes in some detail about his feelings and anecdotes concerning a number of post-strike incidents and events are recounted with a mixture of humour and sadness. The men at Markham Main (Armthorpe, near Doncaster) did not return to work until Friday, 8 March, the last to do so in Yorkshire.

Finally, in pieces written retrospectively, but with considerable perception, Bruce describes his increasing disillusionment with 'pit-work', leading to redundancy and the last shift. Many others will empathise with his feelings and Catch 22 situation.

THE DIARY
The end of the strike.
Monday, 4 March
Meeting at the Baggin. Looks as though the strike has ended but we will be marching back to work from Baggin, with our pit banner tomorrow.

Tuesday, 5 March
I went on the march, from the Silverwood Miners' Welfare (Baggin), then up the hill and on to Silverwood Colliery. On the march I was not upset, just annoyed and bitter; and also had a feeling of being let down – not by the NUM – but by the scabs and people – people in their comfortable jobs in other industries. Mind you, it could be their turn next.

---

1. Bruce Wilson and myself would like to express our thanks to Dave Hadfield ('Wingnut') for information regarding the return to work, by reference to his own diary of events – Editor.

Cortonwood Miners march back to work, March 5th 1985

This commemorative postcard was one of a series produced about the strike and shows Cortonwood miners on their march back to work, 5 March 1985. Yorkshire Evening Post/Judson & Veasey

Wednesday, 6 March

I was due to start back on afternoons, from 12.00 and that morning had to appear at Rotherham Magistrates Court for non-payment of fines. Arrived there early but all the aisles were full of people. I had a word with the usher, telling him it was my first day back at work and I did not want to be late, so he got me in first. The court room was full and I was called to stand in front of the magistrate. He asked me why I had not paid my fines and what my intentions were to pay. There I was, stood with my bread bag in my hand which contained my snap for the afternoon shift. I explained to him that it was my first day back at the pit, on afternoons, after the long strike. The magistrate accepted my offer to pay £1 a week. When he had dealt with me I turned around to walk away but he called out my name. I turned round and he said 'Good luck.' Immediately, a lump came in my throat. It was as if he recognised what we had done. I just could not say anything, just nodded in acknowledgement. I felt very proud.

My first day at Silverwood was spent with my mate Shaun [Bisby] wandering around on the pit top, occasionally sat in the blacksmith's cabin and feeling bored to tears.

As well as returning miners, families and other interested parties came to support the march back to work at Silverwood pit yard, the Union banner in a central position, 5 March 1985.

Only a few men went underground that first shift. Dave Vickers, the pit-bottom loco driver was one of them. According to Dave the pithead baths and certain places on the pit top were 'disgusting', the previous tenants having left discarded food and rubbish all over the place and there was excrement in the showers. Derek Feltham, who worked in the lamproom, came back to find a load of oil lamps missing and some panes of glass broke in the lamproom windows. What caught his attention was that the shards of broken glass were on the floor *outside* the lamproom. You don't have to be Sherlock Holmes to work that one out.

For several days we reported to Silverwood on 'afters' and continued our wanders around the pit top. After this they sent us in buses to Thurcroft Colliery where we went underground. We just got out of the way and sat in the roadways, away from anybody and no one bothered us. An undermanager walked by us, bent down (the roadways were not very high) and just said, 'Morning. You lads from Silverwood?' We just nodded. He never bothered us. We did not like going to Thurcroft as we wanted to get down our own pit.

Back working at Silverwood, I was put on a locomotive. I don't think that many of the men knew what to say or what to think. No one talked about the previous twelve months, as though we had just been on a two-week holiday and were having 'Monday morning blues'. A few times, when I was going into the pit bottom (Braithwell side of the shaft) for supplies, an undermanager would come past. I looked the other way. He looked like Snow White, leading the Seven Dwarfs and would shout out to his followers, 'NOW THEN, SCABBIES, COME ON AND FOLLOW ME' and they would disappear down 18's empty road, to the shaft sump, which was a horrible, damp place – and stay there for several hours. Some of the scabs – you knew them – would sometimes look at you and try to smile. I would look the other way. They started at about 8 am until their shift was done. What a lovely life and existence they had now. When the undermanager called them 'COME ON SCABBIES' we would have got the sack for that. I don't feel sorry for them but I do wonder what they would do if they could turn the clock back.

Friday, 15 March
Drove my car into Thompson's Scrapyard at Parkgate as I had been having some problems with it. I'm working now but still can not afford the repairs. Weighed in for £20. I have to pay the Council for every bit of coke that we had from them, one bag a week.

March [no date]
I saw a local policeman the other day. The last time I saw him was face to face on the picket line at Orgreave, but he just did not want to be there, so he was OK. As I walked up and down the thick formation of police front line you could tell by the look on his face and his nervous acknowledgement of me that he did not like being there.

Aftermath
It was not long before the management exerted their rights to 'manage' and the principles of Thatcher appeared loud and clear for all of us to see. Our union was totally ignored – at least that is how it seemed to me. At the 'top end' some managers started throwing their weight around – you might, for example, get a note on your check at the start of the shift : 'Call and see me at the end of your shift, Mr Wilson – from Personnel Manager'. Then you might be told that your week's hard earned bonus was to be stopped for leaving the pit a few minutes

Another view of the crowded Silverwood pit yard, the Union banner in a central position, 5 March 1985.

early. I'm sure this was an exercise just to show who was the boss. No discussion, just orders and instructions. I disputed my note – and won my case.

When you saw Snow White and the Seven Dwarfs (undermanager and scabs) they never ventured away from the pit bottom and they were treated like lepers, just ignored, although a few of them did try to gain acceptance. Some scabs – well, you did not really hate them – but just thought that they were funny and had not realised what they were doing. In one instance a scab 'management' who we had to work under daily took every insult under the book and never reported us – that's how much he wanted to be accepted. But they never were. One day I came face to face, alone with a scab in the medical centre when I had something in my eye but 'pit humour' came to my rescue on that occasion. I came across one scab many times after work. He would just say, 'Hey up!' not a care in the world. Well, as I've said, some of them did not know any better. I did acknowledge some of the management – they were not worth getting the sack for but they were kept at arms' length.

Things soon got back to 'normal'. Our old district was opened up and Shaun and myself got back to loco driving, taking men and supplies down Braithwell 3 trolley road.

As time moved on I 'wanted out'. Redundancy was on offer and men from the early days of the strike were leaving right, left and centre. No one was left at the pit over 55 years old, then it got to 50. On some days certain jobs could not be manned up, the shortage of manpower was so bad. In the summer of 1987 I put my name down for redundancy and my mate Shaun did the same. I used to look at the list of names of the men that were 'going', every Monday morning. When I used to get my checks out at the start of the shift I would ask in Deployment, 'Any letter for me?' Then, about the middle of November, Shaun, lucky bugger, got his redundancy notice: to finish that week, with twelve week's pay up front, about £1500. I had to wait until the end of February 1988 for my escape letter. I used to count the weeks and days to go. The Personnel manager called me into his office and told me the news and also said that I should work out my present shift for the rest of the week (days), and not to have any time off. I agreed and, as I turned round he said, 'I expect a drink from you!'.

Get on your bike? This cartoon by 'Ken' is worth at least a thousand words on the subject of 'Getting into Nottinghamshire during the 1984–85 miners' strike.' Yorkshire Miner

Two more Brennan cartoons were probably well appreciated by Yorkshire's flying pickets!

Many Orgreave veterans took park in the 2001 re-enactment event. Bob Taylor, with his ever-present cap, is at the centre of the photograph. Courtesy of Jeremy Deller

Bruce and his crew returned to the site of Silverwood colliery in June 2003. Left to right, they are: Bob Wilson, Bob Taylor, Darren Goulty, Bruce Wilson and Shaun Goulty. Brian Elliott

On my last shift I took the men in as usual, talked to all the lads who I had worked with over the years. They were sorry to see me go and I said that I would miss them. I took the manager out on the mail – he was my guard. Reaching the out-bye mail station, I switched the loco off, leaving it for the afternoon shift. The manager walked off. I followed him, looked behind me, down the roadway for the last time, gazing at the roadways and the districts. I knew I would never work down there again. Made my way down to the pit bottom, no rush, taking in all my surroundings and thinking about the many happy memories – our carefree, pre-strike days over.

Near the pit bottom was a stainless steel plaque, about twelve inches long and twelve inches wide, commemorating the Queen's visit to Silverwood in 1975. One or two men had their eyes on that plaque. Men still talked about that royal visit when they white-washed all the coal

There wasn't much left of the old 'Tea Hut' when Bruce (in the easy chair!) and his former flying picket mates visited Silverwood in June 2003. Brian Elliott

seams on her underground route. She rode the Swallow Wood mail, to the end, and rode back, everything whitewashed.

There was no grand entrance or exit for me.

I rode the shaft for the last time.

$\mathcal{A}ppendices$

1 Collieries Referred to in the Diary Entries and main text

NB:

Numbers refer to pages of the book.

Dates refer to year of subsequent closure or privatisation (where known)

Annesley, 61

Babbington, (1986), 54–56, 67, 95

Bentinck, (1994), 51–52, 61, 76, 91–92, 95–96

Bevercotes, (1993), 47, 51, 58–59, 76, 100–101, 111

Blidworth, (1989), 101

Bolsover, 96–97

Brodsworth Main, (1990), 124–26, 129

Brookhouse, (1985), 109, 112–13, 127, 137

Cadley Hill, (1988), 70–71

Calverton, 64

Clipstone, 82–84

Cortonwood, (1985), 41–42, 144, 148–49, 150–54, 158

Cotgrave, (1992), 56, 67

Cresswell, (1991), 47, 50, 57–58, 68, 75–76, 80, 93, 99, 102–103, 111

Dinnington, (1991), 136

Elsecar, (1983), 41

Harworth, 47, 59, 69, 70, 100, 109

Kellingley, 109

Kilnhurst, (1986), 134–35, 141

Kiveton Park, (1994), 105, 108, 112, 123, 124, 129–30

Linby, (1988), 45–47

Maltby, 113–15

Mansfield, (1998), 68, 80

Manton, (1994), 100–101, 137

Markham Main (Derbys), (1993), 96, 101–102

Newstead, (1987), 74–75, 76–77, 97, 100

Ollerton, (1994), 45, 50

Pleasley, (1983), 51, 77

Pye Hill, (1985), 49, 84–85, 89–91, 99

Rossington, 93

Rufford, (1993), 79–80

Sherwood, (1992), 58

Shireoaks, (1990), 127–28

2 Politicians and Officials

BRITTAN, Leon

Born 1939. Conservative politician. Educated Cambridge, Yale & Inner Temple. Chief Secretary at Home Office and Trade Secretary. EU Commissioner in 1988 and later Vice-President.

HEATHFIELD, Peter

Secretary of Derbyshire Area NUM, to 1984 and then General Secretary of the National Union of Mineworkers. Described by Tony Benn as a 'negotiator' and 'diplomat' during the NCB/NUM talks, 7 July 1984.

KINNOCK, Neil

Labour Leader, 1983–92. Born in Gwent, 1942. Degree in Industrial Relations & History at Cardiff. Elected MP for Bedwellty (later Islwyn), 1970. PPR to Michael Foot, 1974–75. Shadow Minister of Education, 1979–83. Resigned after 1992 election defeat. European Commissioner, 1995. Currently Vice-President of the European Commission.

McGAHEY, Mick

President of the Scottish Area NUM, 1967–87. Vice-President of the National Union of Mineworkers, 1973–87, Chairman of Communist Party of Great Britain, 1974–78. One of the three (with Scargill & Heathfield) key miners' union figures during the 1984–85 strike, described as 'a straightforward old statesman' by Tony Benn.

MacGREGOR, Ian

Born Kinlochleven, Scotland, in 1912. Middle class, comfortably off family background. Studied Metallurgy at Glasgow University. 1936–40, worked as a metallurgist in armoury department of Beardmore's on Clydeside. During the war worked in Canada and USA and afterwards stayed, becoming an American citizen and marketing manager of Campbell, Wyat and Cannon. By early 1950s was general manager of Manning, Maxwell & More and had experience of dealing with trade union disputes. Joined board of Climax Molybdenum, countering 'labour problems' there, and later with Amax, both in the context of aluminium, steel and mining. Retired in 1977 but was then involved in US banking. Appointed as non-executive director at troubled British Leyland and, from 1980, moved to British Steel with a similar remit. When he was appointed as chairman of the National Coal Board, on 1 September 1983, he was almost 71-years-old, described by Arthur Scargill as 'that geriatric American butcher'. In his autobiography MacGregor regarded the heroes of the 1984–85 strike as the working miners of Nottinghamshire and the UDM.

NESBIT, John
Former Yorkshire miner who became a senior police officer (Chief Superintendent). Arrested Arthur Scargill at Orgreave. Injured during picket and police confrontation at Maltby Colliery. Speaking to the *Daily Mirror* after the Heseltine pit closure announcement of 1992, he stated that '..a lot of the forecasts made by Scargill … were spot on. You have to concede what he said would happen to the coal industry has come to fruition.'

RICHARDSON, Henry
Nottinghamshire Area NUM President, loyal to the Union during the 1984–85 strike but having to deal with a large membership who continued to work.

SCARGILL, Arthur
Born 1938, Worsbrough Dale, Barnsley. Son of a miner. Worked at Woolley Colliery after leaving school in 1953, starting on the screens and later underground. Young Communist League,1955–62. NUM Branch Committee at Woolley Colliery, 1960 and Delegate, 1964. Came to national prominence during the 1972 miners' strike and the Battle of Saltley Gate when he was a key figure on the Barnsley Area Strike Committee, successfully deploying flying pickets. In 1972 was elected as full-time Yorkshire NUM Compensation Agent, and, shortly afterwards, as President of Yorkshire Miners' Union (1973–81). Had a major role representing the NUM in the enquiries following the Lofthouse (1973) and Houghton Main (1975) colliery disasters. Elected President of the National Union of Minerworkers, 1981, when only 35 years-old. Served for a record 30 years, until 2002. Also President of Miners' Federation of Great Britain and (from 1985) the International Miners' Federation. The last of the great and charismatic miners' leaders of the twentieth century, alongside Herbert Smith, Joe Hall and A J Cook who he much admired. Member of TUC General Council, 1980–83 & 1986–88. Described as 'totally unyielding' and 'a field commander' in a Benn diary entry for 7 July 1984. Fell out with New Labour and founded the Socialist Labour Party (SLP), 1996.

TAYLOR, Jack
Popular and respected Yorkshire Area NUM President during the 1984–85 strike.

THATCHER, Margaret
Born 1925, daughter of a Grantham grocer. Studied at Somerville College, Oxford (Chemistry, and later Law). Worked briefly as a tax lawyer. Elected as Conservative MP for Finchley, 1959 (to 1992). Junior Minister, Pensions & National Insurance, 1961–64, Secretary of State for Education and Science, 1970–74. Leader of Conservative Party, 1975–90. Prime Minister, 1979–90. Her Press Secretary was Bernard Ingram when the 'Maggie Out!' protest became popular. Unemployment reached a 3 million peak in 1982. Her monetarist policy was combined with a reduction in the power of the trade unions. On October 12 1984 she escaped attempted assassination when an IRA bomb was detonated at Brighton's *Grand Hotel* during

the party conference, five people dying following the attack. Introduced the 'community charge' or poll tax in 1989 which resulted in a number of serious riots. Entered House of Lords as Baroness Thatcher of Kesteven, 1992. Continued to be in demand as an international speaker until 2002 when her doctors advised her, on health grounds, to cease public speaking. Volume Two of John Campbell's recent (2003) biography, *The Iron Lady* includes an assessment and account of her activities during the miners' strike of 1984–85.

WALKER, Peter
Born 1932. Conservative politician and leading 'wet' during Thatcher leadership. MP for Worcester, 1961–92. Secretary of State for the Environment, 1970–72 and Trade & Industry, 1972–74. Minister for Agriculture, Fisheries & Food, 1979–83. Energy Secretary during 1984–84 miners' strike. Secretary of State for Wales, 1987–90. Entered House of Lords in 1992.

3 Further Reading

Anon, *A Century of Struggle. Britain's Miners in Pictures 1889–1989,* National Union of Mineworkers, Sheffield,1989

Benn, Tony, *The End of an Era. Diaries 1980–1990*, Hutchinson, London, 1995

Campbell, John, *Margaret Thatcher. Volume Two: The Iron Lady*, Jonathan Cape, London, 2003

Cook, Betty et al, *We Struggled to Laugh*, Barnsley Miners Wives Action Group, Sheffield, 1987

Dolby, Norman, *Account of the Great Miners' Strike*, Verso Books, 1987

Deller, Jeremy, *The English Civil War Part II: personal Accounts of the 1984–85 Miners' Strike*, Artangel, 2001

Douglas, David (compiler), *A Year of our Lives: A Colliery Community* [Hatfield Main] *in the Great Coal Strike of 1984/85*, Hooligan Press, Doncaster, 1986

Douglas David, *All Power to the Imagination/To the Spirit of the Rebel Snowman*, Class War Federation, London, 1999

Dyke, Mel, *All for Barnsley*, Wharncliffe Books, Barnsley, 2003

Elliott, B *Pits and Pitmen of Barnsley*, Wharncliffe Books, Barnsley, 2001

Elliott, B (Ed), *The Miners' Strike Day by Day: The Illustrated 1984–85 Diary of Yorkshire Miner Arthur Wakefield* , Wharncliffe Books, Barnsley, 2002

Fine, Bob & Miller, Robert (eds), *Policing the Miners' Strike*, Lawrence & Wishart, London, 1985

Gibbon, Peter & Steyne, David (eds), *Thurcroft Village and the Miners' Strike*, Spokesman Books, 1986

Glyn, Andrew, *The Economic Case against pit Closures, National Union of Mineworkers*, Sheffield,1984

Hill, Alan, *The South Yorkshire Coalfield. A History and Development*, Tempus Publishing Ltd, Stroud, 2001

Jackson, Bernard, with Wardle, Tony, *The Battle For Orgreave*, Vanson Wardle Productions Ltd, Brighton, 1986

Keating, Jackie, *Counting the Cost: A family in the Miners' Strike*, Wharncliffe Publishing Ltd, Barnsley, 1991

MacGregor, Ian (with Rodney Tyler), *The Enemies Within: The Story of the Miners' Strike 1984–5*, Collins, London, 1985

News Line, *The Miners' Strike 1984–85 in Pictures*, New Park Publications, London, 1985

Ottey, Roy, *The Strike, An Insiders Story*, Sidgewick & Jackson, London, 1987

Reed, David & Adamson, Olivia, *Miners Strike 1984–85: People versus State*, Larkin Publications, London, 1985

Rimington, Stella, *Open Secret. The Autobiography of the Former Director-General of MI5*, Hutchinson, London, 2001

Routledge, Paul, *Scargill. The Unauthorised Biography*, Harper Collins, London, 1993

Seddon, Vicky (ed), *The Cutting Edge: Women and the Pit Strike*, Lawrence & Wishart, London, 1986

Thornton, Jane, *All the Fun of the Fight*, Doncaster Library Service, Doncaster, 1987

Winterton, Jon & Winterton, Ruth, *Coal, Crisis and Conflict:The 1984–85 Miners' Strike in Yorkshire*, Manchester University Press, 1989

4 Acknowledgements

Bruce Wilson and Brian Elliott would like to thank the following individuals and organisations for their help, support and encouragement:

Shaun Bisby; Tim Brannen; Philip Caplan and Philip Howard Books of Rotherham; Eric Cassidy; Jeremy Deller; Judy Ely and Clifton Park Museum, Rotherham; Darren Goulty; Dave Hadfield ('Wingnut'); Keith Lockley ('Corgi'); National Coal Mining Museum for the North of England (Caphouse Colliery, Wakefield); National Union of Mineworkers; Rawmarsh & Parkgate History Group; Granville Richardson; Ricky Tomlinson for sending his good wishes for the book; Brian Ripley; *Rotherham Advertiser*; Rotherham Archives & Local Studies Library; Silverwood Miners' Welfare ('The Baggin'); Silverwood NUM Branch Members; Bob Taylor; Stuart Tennant; Anne Thompson; Dave Vickers; all staff at Wharncliffe & Pen & Sword Books of Barnsley; Anne Whitehouse; Gay Wilson; Bob Wilson; and the *Yorkshire Miner*.

5 Illustrations and credits

Illustrations that are not from Bruce Wilson's camera or collection are, where sources are known credited at the end of each caption.

Index